How to Rescue Your Loved One from the Watchtower

How to Rescue Your Loved One from the Watchtower

David A. Reed

BAKER BOOK HOUSE
Grand Rapids, Michigan 49516

Copyright 1989 by Baker Book House Company

ISBN: 0-8010-7752-4

Third printing, October 1990

Printed in the United States of America

Scripture references

KJV	*King James Version*
LB	*The Living Bible.* © 1971 by Tyndale House Publishers, Wheaton, Illinois 60187.
NEB	*New English Bible.* © 1961 by The Delegates of the Oxford University Press and The Syndics of the Cambridge University Press.
NIV	*The Holy Bible, New International Version.* © 1978 by New York International Bible Society, used by permission of Zondervan Bible Publishers.
NKJV	*New King James Version, Holy Bible.* © 1983 by Thomas Nelson, Inc.
NWT	*New World Translation of the Holy Scriptures.* © 1961, 1981, by Watchtower Bible and Tract Society of Pennsylvania.
RSV	*Revised Standard Version.* © 1946, 1952 by Division of Christian Education of the Churches of Christ in the United States of America.
Goodspeed	Smith-Goodspeed, *The Bible. An American Translation.* Chicago: University of Chicago, 1927, revised 1935.

Contents

Preface

In the summer of 1968, when I had just turned twenty-two years of age, a Jehovah's Witness was assigned to work alongside me at my job. In the course of our introductions I let him know right away that I was an atheist, having decided at the age of fourteen that God was a figment of adult imagination. But I hid from him the fact that I was now re-thinking that position. Existential humanism had already failed me as a philosophy of life, and I found myself forced to think about God again.

Since God was on my mind, I began asking this Witness questions about his beliefs. I expected to hear the same "blind faith" story that had made it easy for me to reject religion eight years earlier. But, instead, his answers amazed me. For the first time I started to hear religious thoughts presented in a tight-knit logical framework. Everything that he said fit together. He had an answer for every question, and so I kept coming up with more questions. Before long he was conducting a study with me twice a week in the Watchtower Society's new (1968) book *The Truth That Leads to Eternal Life* .

In no time, I became a very zealous Witness. After receiving my initial indoctrination and getting baptized, I served as a full-time "pioneer minister." This required that I spend at least one hundred hours each month preaching from house to house and conducting home Bible studies—actually a commitment of much more than a hundred hours, since travel time could not be included in my monthly "field service report." I kept on 'pioneering' until 1971, when I married Penni, who had been raised in the organization and who also "pioneered."

My zeal for Jehovah God and my proficiency in preaching were rewarded, after a few years, with an appointment as an elder. In that capacity I taught the 150-odd people in my home congregation on a regular basis, and made frequent visits to other congregations as a Sunday morning speaker. Occasionally, I also received assignments to speak to audiences ranging in the thousands at Jehovah's Witness conventions.

Other responsibilities included presiding over the other local elders, handling correspondence between our congregation and the Watchtower Society's Brooklyn headquarters, and serving on "judicial committees" set up to judge cases of wrongdoing in the congregation.

Penni, of course, enjoyed the prestige of being a prominent elder's wife. Besides that she was also an excellent teacher in her own right. Although her parents had joined the Witnesses while she was still in grade school, they were "weak in the faith" to the point of sending her to college. (Strong JWs regard higher education as the devil's classroom, as well as a sinful waste of time.) Penni majored in sociology and minored in psychology. After earning her degree at the University of Western Michigan, she went into elementary education. But her talent for teaching applied to adults as well, and she was often used at Kingdom Hall to demonstrate the "right" way to call at homes with the Watchtower message.

Although we were not able to continue "pioneering" after our marriage, Penni and I remained very zealous for the preaching work. Between the two of us, we conducted home Bible studies with dozens of people, and brought more than twenty members into the organization as baptized Jehovah's Witnesses. We also put "the Kingdom" first in our personal lives by keeping our secular employment to a minimum and living in an inexpensive three-room apartment to be able to devote more time to the door-to-door preaching activity.

What interrupted this life of full dedication to the Watchtower organization, and caused us to enter a path that would lead us out? In one word, it was *Jesus*. Let me explain:

When Penni and I were at a large Witness convention, we saw a handful of opposers picketing outside. One of them carried a sign that said, "READ THE BIBLE, NOT THE WATCH-TOWER." We had no sympathy for the picketers, but we did feel convicted by this sign, because we knew that we had been reading Watchtower publications to the exclusion of reading the Bible. (Later we actually counted up all of the material that the organization expected Witnesses to read. The books, magazines, lessons, etc., added up to over three thousand pages each year, compared with less than two hundred pages of Bible reading assigned—and most of that was in the Old Testament. The majority of Witnesses were so bogged down by the three thousand pages of the organization's literature that they never got around to reading the Bible.)

After seeing the picket sign Penni turned to me and said, "We should be reading the Bible AND *The Watchtower*." I agreed; so, we began doing regular personal Bible reading.

That's when we began to focus on Jesus. Not that we began to question the Watchtower's teaching that Christ was just Michael the archangel in human flesh! It didn't even occur to us to question that. But we were really impressed with Jesus as a person: what he said and did, how he treated people. We wanted to be his followers.

Especially we were struck with how Jesus responded to the hypocritical religious leaders of the day, the scribes and Pharisees. I remember reading over and over again the accounts relating how the Pharisees objected to Jesus' healing on the Sabbath, his disciples' eating with unwashed hands, and other minor details of behavior that violated their traditions. How I loved Jesus' response: "You hypocrites, Isaiah aptly prophesied about you, when he said, 'This people honors me with their lips, yet their heart is far removed from me. It is in vain that they keep worshiping me, because they teach commands of men as doctrines'" (Matt. 15:7-9 NWT).

Commands of men as doctrines! That thought stuck in my mind. And I began to realize that, in fulfilling my role as a JW elder, I was acting more like a Pharisee than a follower of Jesus. For example, the elders were the enforcers of all sorts of petty rules about dress and grooming. We told sisters how long they could wear their dresses, and we told brothers how to comb their hair, how short to trim their sideburns, and what sort of flare or taper they could wear in their pantlegs. We actually told people that they could not please God unless they conformed. It reminded me of the Pharisees who condemned Jesus' disciples for eating with unwashed hands.

When my fellow elders stopped a young man from doing the door-to-door preaching work because he had grown a goatee, my conscience would not allow me to continue giving tacit approval to such "commands of men." But, rather than get into a battle of words, I decided to imitate Jesus' example of healing on the Sabbath. I chose to break the tradition of the elders by combing my hair over the tops of my ears.

Penni became frightened and upset. Even if she no longer believed that my relationship with God depended on having an approved "theocratic haircut," she knew that others in the congregation were bound by the traditions I was challenging. And she knew that the organization was very powerful.

Penni was right. I soon found myself on trial before the elders for the half-inch of hair over the tops of my ears. The Circuit Overseer who prosecuted me brought in congregation members to testify as eyewitnesses to this "sin." As my trials and ensuing appeals dragged on for weeks and then months, I had to sit down with Penni many times to discuss with her what I was doing and why. Grooming was not the real issue. It was a question of whose disciple I was. Was I a follower of Jesus, or an obedient servant to a human hierarchy?

The elders who put me on trial knew that that was the real issue, too. They kept asking, "Do you believe that the Watchtower Society is God's organization? Do you believe that the Society speaks as Jehovah's mouthpiece?"

At that time I answered *Yes* because I still did believe it was God's organization—but that it had become corrupt, like the Jewish religious system at the time when Jesus was opposed by the Pharisees. Soon, however, I began to realize that the Watchtower Society never did represent God as his organization on earth. Then I had to help Penni step-by-step to reach the same conclusion. It seemed that I was always a few steps ahead of her in this process. But I was careful not to move ahead so fast as to let her slip behind. (When one mate leaves the JWs and the other remains in the sect, the result is often a bitter divorce.) Close daily communication was essential.

Eventually, it was no longer my grooming but what I said at

the congregation meetings that got me into real trouble. I was still an elder, so, when I was assigned to give a fifteen-minute talk on the Book of Zechariah at the Thursday night Theocratic Ministry School meeting, I took advantage of the opportunity to encourage the audience to read the Bible. In fact, I told the members that, if their time was limited and they had to choose between reading the Bible and reading *The Watchtower* magazine, they should choose the Bible, because it was inspired by God while *The Watchtower* was not inspired and often taught errors that had to be corrected later. Not surprisingly, that was the last time they allowed me to give a talk.

When they also stopped handing me the microphone to speak from my seat during the Sunday morning question-and-answer *Watchtower* lesson, I responded by publishing a newsletter titled *Comments from the Friends.* I wrote articles questioning what the organization was teaching, and signed them with the pen name Bill Tyndale, Jr.—a reference to sixteenth-century English Bible translator William Tyndale, who was burned at the stake for what he wrote. To avoid getting caught, Penni and I drove at night to an out-of-state post office and mailed the articles in unmarked envelopes. We sent them to local Witnesses and also to hundreds of Kingdom Halls all across the country.

Penni and I knew that we had to leave the Jehovah's Witnesses. But, to us, it was similar to the question of what to do in a burning apartment building. Do you escape through the nearest exit? Or do you bang on doors first, waking the neighbors and helping them escape, too? We felt an obligation to help others get out—especially our families and the converts that we had brought into the organization. If we had simply walked out, our families left behind would have been forbidden to associate with us.

But, after a few weeks a friend discovered what I was doing and turned me in. So one night when Penni and I were returning home from conducting a Bible study, two men in trench coats got out of a parked car and began walking toward us. When they stepped under a streetlight, we recognized them as two of the elders. They questioned me about the newsletter and wanted to put me on trial for publishing it, but we simply stopped attending Kingdom Hall. By that time most of our former friends there had become quite hostile toward us. One young man called on the phone and threatened to "come over and take care of" me if he got another one of our newsletters. And another Witness actually left a couple of death threats on our answering machine. The elders went ahead and tried us *in absentia* and expelled us from the congregation.

It was a great relief to be out from under the oppressive yoke of that organization. But we now had to face the immediate challenge of where to go and what to believe. It takes some time to re-think one's entire religious outlook on life. Before leaving the Watchtower, we had rejected the claims that the organization was God's "channel of communication", that Christ returned invisibly in the year 1914, and that the "great crowd" of believers since 1935 should not partake of the communion loaf and cup. But, we were only beginning to re-examine other doctrines. And we had not yet come into fellowship with Christians outside the JW organization.

All Penni and I knew was that we wanted to follow Jesus and that the Bible contained all the information we needed. So, we really devoted ourselves to reading the Bible and to prayer. We also invited our families and remaining friends to meet in our apartment on Sunday mornings. While the Witnesses gathered at Kingdom Hall to hear a lecture and study *The Watchtower*, we met to read the Bible. As many as fifteen attended—mostly family, but some friends also.

We were just amazed at what we found in prayerfully reading the New Testament over and over again—things that we had never appreciated before, such as the closeness that the early disciples had with the risen Lord, the activity of the Holy Spirit in the early church, and Jesus' words about being born again. In time, all of these things came to be reflected in our own experience, as we embraced genuine Christianity.

Penni teaches fifth grade now in a Christian school that has students from about twenty different churches. She really enjoys it, because she can integrate the Scriptures with academic subjects. And I continue publishing *Comments from the Friends* as a sixteen-page quarterly for ex-Witnesses and persons with JW friends or relatives. Subscribers are found in a score of foreign countries, as well as across the United States and Canada. Besides writing on the subject, I speak occasionally to church groups interested in learning how to answer Jehovah's Witnesses.

Looking back, I realize that I was truly blessed in helping escape from the Watchtower not only my dear wife, but also her parents, my three brothers, and most of my in-laws—not to mention numerous other former JWs encountered since then in public ministry. But in all these cases I am convinced that I merely assisted as an instrument while the rescue was actually accomplished by the Lord Jesus Christ of whom it is said, "if the Son sets you free, you will be free indeed" (John 8:36 NIV).

Introduction

Ever since becoming involved with Christian outreach to Jehovah's Witnesses, I have received a steady stream of mail from persons who have a marriage mate, relative, or friend in the Watchtower organization. Invariably these letters express dismay at the loved one's involvement with the sect, coupled with a sense of frustration after unsuccessful attempts to persuade them to quit.

In the case of a married couple what typically happens is this: The husband initially hears that his wife is "studying the Bible with two nice ladies who come to the house every Wednesday afternoon." He may answer with a casual "That's nice, dear." Or, he may say, "Fine, as long as I don't have to get involved!" But the reaction is usually one of disinterested toleration—that is, until he finds out that the ladies are Jehovah's Witnesses and that his wife will soon be joining them in door-to-door sales of *Watchtower* magazines, attending meetings at Kingdom Hall Sunday mornings and two nights a week, teaching the kids not to celebrate birthdays or Christmas, and carrying a card in her purse advising medical personnel not to administer blood if she is found unconscious and hemorrhaging.

Many a husband's disinterested toleration then gives way to violent opposition. He calls the Jehovah's Witnesses everything from cultists to communists. While the "two nice ladies" coach the wife on how to answer his objections with arguments he is unable to refute, the husband finds himself resorting to shouts and curses. He knows the Watchtower is wrong, but lacks the ammunition to prove it. He feels himself ready to explode as he watches his wife become more and more wrapped up with the organization, impervious to his attempts to dissuade her.

At this point a crossroads is reached. Feeling defeated and not wanting to lose touch with his wife, the man may decide to accompany her to Kingdom Hall meetings and to sit in on a "Bible study" to be conducted with the two of them by a JW elder and his wife. Or, at the other extreme, the husband may separate from his wife, initiate divorce proceedings, and attempt to take custody of the children. Many husbands take one of these two opposite courses. In between, however, there are many others who simply attempt to ride out the storm. They stop talking about religion to avoid the inevitable arguments, and they try to maintain some semblance of family life in spite of the spouse's heavy schedule of meeting attendance and door-to-door work and her avoidance of family gatherings normally held on such occasions as Easter, Mother's Day, Father's Day, and Thanksgiving—holidays the Witnesses attack as "pagan celebrations." The marriage stays together, but the wife's religion remains a source of irritation and tension.

I have seen all of the above happen in innumerable cases, but perhaps the most universal expression I have heard from men in every one of those situations is this: "I love my wife deeply, but somehow she seems to have become a different person. It's as if there is an invisible wall between us."

Although ordinarily it is the wife who is found at home and is therefore contacted by "two nice ladies" calling from house to house, sometimes it is the husband who is initially drawn into the Watchtower organization, perhaps through a workmate or business associate. When this happens, the effect on marriage and homelife is just as disastrous.

And a similar sort of estrangement occurs when the one joining the Witnesses is a son or daughter, a parent, a brother or sister, or even a close friend. It seems that the new JW loses interest in the former relationship, maintaining contact only insofar as this means opportunities to preach Watchtower doctrine. The good times together are gone, and there is a well-founded fear that if the door is closed to further "preaching" the relationship may end altogether.

After spending years writing letters to people desperate to

rescue their loved ones from the Watchtower—all the while wishing that the letters could be longer and more detailed—wishing that I could write each one a book instead of a mere letter—I have finally forced myself to take the time out from a busy schedule to actually write such a book.

In responding to letters, of course, I have often made use of existing tools in the field of cult ministry, and have sent those in need a volume on JW doctrine, a collection of testimonies by former Witnesses, a book on the Watchtower organization's history or a copy of my own book *Jehovah's Witnesses Answered Verse by Verse* , but none of these in itself could serve as a complete guide to rescuing a loved one from the sect. Although these books provide the raw material needed for such an effort, none of them combines this with a step-by-step strategy. And even books aimed at equipping Christians to answer JWs at the door do not detail the best approach to take when the Witness is a member of the household or a close friend.

With over eight million people attending JW Kingdom Halls worldwide, including close to two million here in the United States, and new converts being made at the rate of four thousand per week, there is a growing need for assistance to their millions of non-Witness family members, relatives and friends. The methods outlined in these pages enabled me to lead my wife out of the Watchtower (while I myself was in the process of leaving, a few steps ahead of her), and they have proved successful in helping many others to do the same. Of course the choice ultimately lies within the free will of each human heart faced with the option of believing a lie or accepting the truth. One Witness woman actually told me, "Even if someone could prove to me beyond doubt that the organization was false, I would still stick with it." (She evidently had her own motives for this.) So, there can be no guarantee that this book, used correctly, will produce the desired result.

Few who join the Watchtower have this woman's attitude, however; most truly believe that they have found the way to God's approval, and if shown that the organization's claims in this regard are false, these individuals will gladly quit, breathing a sigh of relief. I have seen it happen time and again. Therefore I am confident that this book will prove helpful in many cases to those who want to rescue a loved one from the Watchtower.

1

"Rescue" from a Religion?

We speak of "rescue" when someone is trapped in a burning building, adrift at sea, or held captive by kidnappers, but we usually do not speak of "rescuing" someone from a religion. So, although anyone who has a family member, relative or friend in the Watchtower organization will immediately understand why we use this term in our title, it should be explained for the benefit of others.

Those trapped in a place that they can not get out of by themselves may need rescue. The Watchtower is such a place, because members of the sect are not free to leave. If a member decides to walk away from the group, he is summoned before a judicial committee made up of three or more elders from his local congregation. They ask him to give them a "letter of disassociation"—a signed confession to the crime of leaving the organization—and, if he will not do so, the elders on the committee meet together and weigh the evidence before reaching the verdict that he has committed that crime. In either case at the next congregation meeting a public announcement is made to the effect that "so-and-so has disassociated himself from Jehovah's organization and is no longer one of Jehovah's Witnesses." The remaining members are then called on to punish the offender by avoiding any contact with him. They are not even to say *hello* if they encounter him on the street. Fear of receiving this treatment acts as a deterrent to JWs who might otherwise leave the sect.

A Jehovah's Witness who contemplates leaving the organization knows that he risks losing his JW wife, his children, his parents, and any other relatives or close friends in the faith. Family members living in the same household are required to cut off "spiritual fellowship" with the former Witness, while those living outside the home are advised to "have almost no contact with the relative. Even if there were some family matters requiring contact, this certainly would be kept to a minimum . . ." (*The Watchtower*, 4/15/88, p. 28). I am in regular personal contact with a number of men who very much want to leave the organization, but who do not take this action for fear of losing their wives and children. I know a grandmother who wants to speak out against the sect, but who fears this will mean an end to her visits with the grandchildren. From these individuals' point of view, their religious organization is in effect holding their relatives hostage. Rescue is definitely in order.

Real-life drama grips the nation when news media report an injured child trapped at the bottom of a well or miners cut off by a cave-in. Police and fire departments have rescue teams trained to scale walls, if necessary, to bring life-saving medical help to those in need. In the case of Jehovah's Witnesses there is an invisible wall preventing them from receiving blood transfusions, even when their lives or the lives of their children depend on it. True, the "wall" exists in their own minds and in an organizational structure that will put them on trial if they accept a needed transfusion, but they need rescue just as much as if trapped behind walls of wood or concrete.

In the case of people held hostage by armed terrorists or trapped by fire or fallen rock, rescue attempts are often risky. The very effort to reach them might easily trigger further harm with perhaps fatal consequences. And in the case of Jehovah's Witnesses there is a similar risk involved. The would-be rescuer, hitherto viewed simply as an outsider to the sect, could suddenly be seen as an "opposer" who must be avoided as "bad association." The relationship that had been deteriorating due to the sect's influence might now be severed entirely in response to a command from the local elders. So the rescue attempt is something that is not to be viewed lightly nor to be undertaken carelessly or without regard to the inherent risks. Preparation should be made carefully and prayerfully before assaulting the Watchtower fortress.

2

Don't Delay—Act Today!

As the adage says, "An ounce of prevention is worth a pound of cure." It is usually much easier to free an individual from the Watchtower if his or her involvement can be nipped in the bud. During the first few days or weeks of contact the newly interested individual may be motivated mostly by curiosity. At this stage it is easy to debunk the organization by refuting its errors and exposing its embarrassing history. Do so at once, without delay.

As each new Watchtower doctrine is "proved" to the prospective convert and accepted as a valid belief, another step is added to the process that will eventually be required to undo the effects of this indoctrination. And the odds that this can be accomplished at all are made slimmer. Once the "churches of Christendom" are discredited in the first few lessons, it will later take time and effort to reestablish the fact that there exist genuine Christians outside the Watchtower organization. Once another early lesson teaches that God must be addressed as "Jehovah" in prayer, it will be difficult for the student to pray again without using that formula. Once the Witnesses "prove" that the dead go neither to heaven nor to hell but are unconscious and nonexistent, that thought will remain unless answered in detail from Scripture. And once the student is convinced by his or her JW teacher that the Watchtower Society is "God's organization" and "the channel of communication that God is using," extricating the new convert grows into a major project, requiring intense effort, assistance from trained personnel, and perhaps months or years of patient endurance.

The act of baptism represents an outward commitment to join the organization and abide by its rules. However since group baptisms are usually held just two or three times a year, most individuals make an inward commitment, intellectually and emotionally, months before baptism. If you are able to intervene before such a commitment is made, stress the need to examine "the other side of the story" first, especially before publicly accepting the responsibilities of membership. Tell the baptismal candidate that he or she owes it you, to himself and to God, to find out why other sincere, committed members have left the organization, and why the group seeks to prevent members from reading books ex-members have written.

If, on the other hand, your loved one has already recently been baptized, the problem becomes a bit more complex. Showing him that the Watchtower is wrong now carries with it, by implication, the additional thought that he himself was wrong in publicly dedicating himself to the group. People do not like to admit that they have made a mistake, so this makes matters more difficult. You may be able to sidestep the problem, though, by saying something like this: "I know that you joined the Witnesses because everything they told you sounded good. But you never really had a chance to hear the other side of the story. They hid from you certain facts that might have affected your decision had you known about them. Before you get more deeply involved, you really owe it to yourself to examine this material that I have collected. Wouldn't it be better to look at it now than after you have spent most of your life working for the Watchtower?"

Once someone becomes fully established as a new member, he or she typically enters a "honeymoon" period during which it becomes almost impossible to penetrate his thinking. He has just made a public commitment and is surrounded by fellow Witnesses who commend him for his choice and shower him with love and attention. At this stage the best thing you can do may simply be to keep open the lines of communication and to keep reaffirming your love and personal interest. It may take a year or more before the other JWs stop regarding the convert as "a new one" in need of special treatment. When the honeymoon is finally over and the new one comes to be regarded as just another member of the congregation, that is when disillusionment with the sect can start to set in. Depending on how perceptive the individual is, he or she will sooner or later begin to realize that there is a lot of playacting going on and that fellow Witnesses have a lot of problems. When it finally hits home that there is no real love in the organization, your patiently keeping open lines of communication and confirming your love may start to bear fruit—but this may be a long time in coming.

So, the main point to remember when a loved one first starts getting involved with Jehovah's Witnesses is to *avoid delay*. As in fighting an infectious disease that attacks the body, time is of the essence in combating the Watchtower's invasion of the mind.

The need for speed is highlighted by the fact that one of the first lessons taught by the Witnesses usually includes a warning against relatives who may try to stop the study:

> How might Satan even use friends and relatives to discourage us? . . .
> You can be sure that Satan the Devil does not want you to have this knowledge, and that he will do all in his power to stop you from getting it. How will he do this? One way is by seeing to it that you receive opposition, perhaps in the form of ridicule. . . . It may be that even close friends or relatives will tell you that they do not like your examining the Scriptures. Jesus Christ himself even warned: "Indeed, a man's enemies will be persons of his own household. . . ." . . . But if you give up a study of God's Word when opposition comes, how will God view you? (*You Can Live Forever in Paradise on Earth*, Watchtower Society, 1982, p. 23.)

If the new student accepts this argument, chances of stopping the study dim immediately. If you come along at this point with objections, you already have two strikes against you: (1) you appear to be an instrument of Satan the devil, so the arguments you present are viewed with suspicion and skepticism; and (2) by fulfilling the Witnesses' prophecy that a close friend or relative would oppose the study, you have made them appear to be true prophets. If the objections you raise at this point are weak or are poorly presented, and therefore are overcome by the JWs,

you will have struck out. Unless some powerful evidence
against the sect is quickly brought into play at this time, the
game is over, at least for now.

Perhaps the mistake most commonly made in attempting to
rescue a potential convert is failure to act soon enough. If you
can jump in at the very beginning, the best advice would be to do
something—to do almost anything— that will stop the study in
a kind, loving manner. Even a stalling tactic will help, if it will
allow you time to study the evidence against the cult and better
prepare your defense. Persuade your wife to postpone the study
until next week, so that you can take her out to eat, or invite
relatives over for a visit, or schedule something else that will
interfere with the study "just this one time"—and in the mean-
time, prepare your case against the Witnesses.

On the other hand, if the study has already been in progress
for some time, you will have to proceed with extra caution. You
do not want to fulfill the JWs prophecy that the devil would use
you to torpedo the discussions. This would make you look like
the "bad guy" and would vindicate the Witnesses. At this point
a harsh ultimatum that your wife *must* break off with the JWs
could have disastrous results. And a series of unsupported, non-
factual accusations (such as the often quoted but misinformed
charges that they are communists, that they do not love their
children, or that they refuse all medical treatment) will do a lot
more harm than good. If the Witnesses can disprove the initial
charges you bring against them, they may be able to persuade
their student not to listen to any future accusations. It is very
important to have all your arguments correct and fully documented the first time around; otherwise, there may not be a
second chance.

While a brand new student can be told, "Look! I have collected a pile of material that will demonstrate to you that the
Watchtower Society is a false prophet," one who is more fully
involved and has been under JW influence for some time must
be approached more delicately. Such a bold, direct approach
would be too frightening, giving rise to the thought that you
could be an "opposer" sent by Satan the devil. It would be less
intimidating if you put it this way: "On account of your interest
in it, I have been investigating the Watchtower, too, and I have

found some information I want to share with you. I would like to get your opinion of what this says."

In any case, you should definitely avoid attempting to disprove the Watchtower to a new student with the JW teacher present. This will only turn into a free-for-all debate, with the longtime JW coming up with an answer, excuse or denial for everything you say. And, unless you are thoroughly versed on the Watchtower Society and well trained as a debater, the JW recruiter will shoot you down on every point. He will be the winner, and the new student will be further cemented into the sect. So when you sit down with your loved one to discuss the sect, be sure to exclude the Jehovah's Witness teacher from being there. Meet with your loved one alone, or, if possible, arrange to have with you a former Witness or another individual specially trained in combating cultic mind-control.

It is important to plan your strategy, collect convincing evidence, and present it in the proper manner at an appropriate time. The remaining chapters of this book will help you do just that.

3

Overall Strategy

Atypical encounter between a Christian and a Jehovah's Witness goes like this: The Christian shows the JW a Bible verse that contradicts Watchtower teaching. The JW then responds with another verse that he feels supports his beliefs. The Christian then counters with another verse, to which the JW replies with still another, and so forth. Such a discussion can be described as "biblical Ping-Pong." Verses bounce back and forth, perhaps for hours on end, with no tangible results other than the sweaty exhaustion that follows a literal Ping-Pong game. And even if the Christian seems to have come off the "winner" in the debate, this carries no more weight with the Jehovah's Witness than if it had been a mere Ping-Pong game he had lost; he is still not about to change his religion.

What is wrong with the above approach? Why does a well-planned barrage of Bible verses usually fail to make a dent in a Witness's thinking? The reason is that this form of attack is based upon a wrong assumption. It assumes that the Jehovah's Witness believes certain things on account of what he has read in the Bible, and that he will change his beliefs if he is shown other verses as prooftexts for a different doctrinal stance. But anyone making this assumption has already fallen victim to the sect's propaganda: namely, the claim that Jehovah's Witnesses are Bible-reading people who rely on Scripture as their highest authority. Actually they do little personal Bible reading aside from looking up isolated verses cited in Watchtower literature.

And they base their beliefs, not on what they find in the Bible, but on what their leaders tell them the Bible says.

For example, consider what happened on one occasion when two ladies called at my door with *Watchtower* and *Awake!* magazines in their hands. I let the one taking the lead go ahead with her presentation for a minute or two, rejected her offer of the magazines, but then asked if she could answer a Bible question for me before she left. (Jehovah's Witnesses love to "teach" people they meet in their door-to-door work by answering Bible questions—especially since they think they know all the answers.) My question was this: Where do you find in the Bible your belief that "the great crowd" of true worshipers today will be rewarded with everlasting life on earth instead of in heaven? She promptly flipped open the pages of her *New World Translation* and showed me Revelation 7:9, "After these things I saw, and, look! a great crowd, which no man was able to number, out of all nations and tribes and peoples and tongues, standing before the throne and before the Lamb, dressed in white robes; and there were palm branches in their hands."

When I showed her the context and pointed out that the "great crowd" is pictured there "standing before the throne" of God in heaven, rather than on earth, she answered that all the earth stands before God's throne. So I had her turn over a few pages to Revelation, chapter 19, which also speaks of the "great crowd," and asked her to read the first verse: "After these things I heard what was as a loud voice of a great crowd in heaven. They said, 'Praise Jah, you people! The salvation and the glory and the power belong to our God.' "

"So, where is the 'great crowd'?" I asked.

"On earth," was her reply.

"Please read it again," I asked.

She did, but this time I stopped her after the word *heaven* and asked again where the verse located the "great crowd."

"On earth," was still her answer.

Then I got her to look at Revelation 19:1 again and admit that she had read the word *heaven.*

"It says 'heaven'," she finally acknowledged, "but the 'great crowd' is on earth. You don't understand," she went on, "we have men at our headquarters in Brooklyn, New York, who explain the Bible to us. And they can prove that the 'great crowd' is on earth; I just can't explain it that well."

By this admission she revealed the true nature of the problem. She made it clear that her belief was based, not on what the Bible said, but on what her leaders said it said—even to the point that she could look at the word *heaven* and see *earth* instead. Most people would call this brainwashing.

This explains why a barrage of Bible verses can bounce off a Jehovah's Witness like so many Ping-Pong balls, with no effect. The JW may look at the verses, but what he sees in his mind's eye is the Watchtower Society's *interpretation* of those verses. It is as if he is looking at the pages of the Bible through Watchtower-colored glasses. So the first step in your strategy must be to remove those distorted lenses. To accomplish this, you will have to get the Witness to look at the Watchtower organization itself. You will need to demonstrate that the leaders have made repeated false prophecies, have changed doctrines back and forth, and have misled followers to their harm—that is, they are *not* a reliable guide to follow. The Witness will then be forced to think for himself or herself; in effect, the Watchtower-colored glasses will be removed.

But this can be difficult, because JWs are trained to keep opening the Bible, bringing up prooftexts for their various teachings. And your natural response would be to answer them on each point. As long as you allow them to control the discussion in this way, though, they will never see the forest for the trees, as the expression goes. At some point you must interrupt the issue-by-issue argument to focus attention on the big issue, the organization itself.

Picture the Watchtower, for a moment, as an ancient walled fort with archers and spearmen standing guard atop the wall. Your army surrounds the fort. Your archers shoot arrows at their counterparts on the wall, and your spearmen hurl missiles. Sometimes your men score a hit, and sometimes theirs do; but the battle goes nowhere. Nowhere, that is, until a contingent of your men stop trading shots with the enemy and instead, with helmets on their heads, shields on their backs and shovels in their hands, dig around the base of the wall until it is undermined and collapses. As it falls, so do the host of archers and spearmen who stood atop it, seemingly invulnerable only moments before.

Disputing with a Jehovah's Witness over questions of deity, theology, and the afterlife can be like the archers and spearmen exchanging shots with those on the wall. But attacking the organization itself, destroying its credibility by exposing its long history of error—this is akin to undermining the wall and causing it to topple over. When the organization falls, so do all the teachings and doctrines that depend on its authority for support.

It will take discipline on your part to ignore some of the "spears" and "arrows" thrown at you in the form of doctrinal challenges, in order to focus your attention and the attention of the Witness on the organization itself; but it will be well worth the effort. Once the organization's authority is undermined, the doctrines will be much easier to deal with.

Before considering the ammunition to fire against the Watchtower organization, however, you would be wise to learn some techniques that work and to familiarize yourself with the tools you will need to use.

4

Techniques that Work

Consider the story of Henry.

When Henry discovered that his wife was already deeply involved with the Jehovah's Witnesses and was in fact about to be baptized as a full-fledged member, he began doing research to accumulate evidence against the Watchtower Society and its teachings. After a month of intense effort he had gathered together six books, twelve cassette tapes, two dozen tracts and a hundred pages of notes. He was now ready to present the evidence to his wife. Knowing that she was about to return home from the Tuesday night Congregation Book Study meeting, he assembled his materials and waited for her in the front hallway, half-way up the stairs. When he heard the sound of her key in the lock, he picked up all his materials, and as she entered the hall and turned to face him, he swung his arms in the air and flung everything he had at her. All at once she was engulfed in a hailstorm of books and tapes, followed by a flurry of notepapers and tracts.

"See! The Watchtower is wrong! wrong! wrong!" Henry shouted at her, as his wife beat a hasty retreat to the car.

She returned to the Kingdom Hall just in time, before the elders had locked it up for the night, and asked them to find her temporary lodging so she could take refuge from her husband's "vicious persecution."

This parable of Henry and his wife is a fictitious story, but it is not far off from describing what actually happens in many cases.

Though not literally dumping books and tapes on a Witness's head, overzealous friends or relatives will often bombard a JW with facts, figures, quotes, and Bible verses in rapid-fire succession. And the results are usually as disastrous as in Henry's case.

The would-be rescuer has no trouble receiving all that information, because each new point is a welcome addition to the arsenal of facts he is collecting to support his contention. The Witness, on the other hand, sees each point as a strange and frightening new thought, a scary challenge to cherished beliefs. Someone unaccustomed to "independent thinking" finds it difficult to entertain even one unfamiliar notion, never mind a surging flood of foreign ideas. And this flash flood of ideas threatens to wash away the Witness's faith and undermine the structure of his universe.

Cult members aside, the ordinary person can absorb only so much new information at one time. Especially is this true when the data appears not to fit in with, or even to contradict, other data already stored in the brain. The mind needs time to analyze the new information, look at it from all angles, and decide which of the contrary notions ought to be stored for future use and which ought to be discarded as useless rubbish. This process can not be rushed, especially when the push comes from someone else who is trying to force-feed new concepts.

A gardener will appreciate that even though a dry plot of land may be dying of thirst, a sudden heavy downpour does more harm than good: instead of penetrating the soil, the pouring rain just runs off, washing away topsoil and perhaps even newly planted seed. What is needed to relieve the drought is gentle rain—even just a sprinkle at first—repeated often and over a long period of time.

Naturally anyone with a close friend or relative trapped in a cult wants to get that person out as soon as possible. So the temptation is strong to act quickly and forcefully, pouring out as much evidence as can be obtained, all at once, and with great gusto. Indeed that may be the best course to take when a loved one is *just beginning* to get involved with a cult; it may be just what is needed to scare them off from further involvement. But it is generally *not* the advisable course when the cultist is already fully involved and has been for some time. Such an individual is likely to be scared off *from you* and to run back to the cult for the comfort of familiar surroundings.

The point is that getting someone out of a controlling sect is not a quick job, like pulling a tooth. The process of extraction can be expected to take some time. Techniques must be used that will allow you to work gradually over a period of time.

In the case of Jehovah's Witnesses even more is required than simply to "go slow." It is also necessary to "play dumb." This is because the Watchtower Society has forewarned its followers that attempts will be made to dissuade them from their beliefs, and the organization has instructed them to avoid anyone who appears bent on accomplishing that end. As already mentioned, early-on in their "free home Bible study" Jehovah's Witnesses tell their students that Satan the devil is likely to use friends or relatives in an attempt to get them to "stop examining the Scriptures" (*You Can Live Forever in Paradise on Earth*, pp. 22-23). So, if you tell the new "student" that you think he ought to stop studying with the Witnesses, you (1) make the JW's look like true prophets, because you fulfilled their prediction that you would act that way; and (2) you identify yourself as someone under the influence of Satan the devil and opposed to God. Watchtower leaders have intentionally planted these thoughts in the minds of new "students" in order to head off any attempt by friends or relatives to stop the study.

Now if persons who are only in the second chapter of their first book are already being conditioned to view opposition to the Watchtower as originating with the devil, just think of how those must feel who have been exposed to years of indoctrination from the study of dozens of books and hundreds of magazines, plus five hours of meetings each week! They can almost see Satan standing behind you, the opposer, manipulating you and speaking through you.

Every so often we hear on the evening news that a firebug has set fire to a building, destroying property and endangering lives. Usually, however, most of the intended victims managed to escape because they heeded the sound of fire alarms or the shouts of their neighbors. But suppose for a moment that a more calculating pyromaniac were to dress himself in a business suit and calmly knock at each door in a hotel or apartment building, warning the residents to "Please, remain inside your unit, because a sniper is on the loose. The sniper's method is to sound a fire alarm and then shoot at people as they flee into the hallways or onto the balconies. Regardless of what you hear, don't open your door, or the sniper will get you." Then the firebug proceeds to set the building on fire and leave. The alarm sounds, but people remain in their units with the doors shut. An off-duty fireman sees smoke and enters the building before any engines arrive. He starts pounding on doors calling, "Fire! Fire! Evacuate the building!" but the people inside remain silent or else shout, "Go away!" An off-duty policeman joins him and kicks down the door of a unit where he saw children peeking out the window. But the father, determined to save his family from the "sniper," fires a rifle at the open door. In self-defense, the policeman returns the fire. Now others in the building who had begun to think of leaving change their mind. The warning was correct; there really is a sniper—they heard the shots.

The frustration faced by these would-be rescuers illustrates the situation of anyone trying to rescue a friend or relative from the Watchtower: the harder you try to help, the more the Witness resists. The more forcefully you attempt to effect a rescue, the more convinced the JW becomes that Satan has sent you.

So, there is no alternative other than to *conceal* the fact that your aim is to get the individual out of the organization. To do otherwise would almost certainly doom your effort to failure.

When dealing with someone who has only recently started to study with the Jehovah's Witnesses, but who has already been warned that the devil will use friends and relatives against him, you might try an approach like this:

I'm glad to see that you are really sincere about wanting to know God and to do his will. I feel the same way myself. Of course, it's a serious matter to commit oneself to a particular religious organization, and I would want to be absolutely certain before taking such a serious step. So I have begun investigating the Jehovah's Witnesses, too, looking at *both* sides of the story. I mean that there is much to be said in favor of the group, but there is also much in their history that makes me see the need for caution. They paint a rosy picture of themselves, but I'm afraid they may be telling only part of the story. And when they instruct people not to read anything by persons who left the group, it's enough to make you wonder if they may have something to hide. In fact, I found some interesting information in this [book/or tape]. Here—perhaps you would like to [read/or listen to] it. I'm sure you, too, want to know all the facts before you get so deeply involved that they can tell you not to listen to anything else.

That approach may open the door to reach someone newly studying with the Witnesses. It will not work with those who have already become "dedicated and baptized" or who have been undergoing indoctrination for a long period of time. They have been fed a steady diet of warnings such as these:

Beware of those who try to put forward their own contrary opinions (*The Watchtower* 3/15/86, p. 17). Do you refuse to listen to bitter criticism of Jehovah's organization? You should refuse (*The Watchtower*, 5/15/84, p. 17).

Avoid Independent Thinking
. . . How is such independent thinking manifested? A common way is by questioning the counsel that is provided by God's visible organization. (*The Watchtower*, 1/15/83, p. 22).

Fight Against Independent Thinking
. . . And just as in the first century there was only one true Christian organization so today Jehovah is using only one organization. (Ephesians 4:4,5; Matthew 24:45–47). Yet there are some who point out that the organization has had to make adjustments before, and so they argue: "This shows that we have to make up our own mind on what to believe." This is independent thinking. Why is it so dangerous? Such thinking is an evidence of pride (*The Watchtower*, 1/15/83, p. 27).

Although a Jehovah's Witness who believes that these instructions are from God will go up to the door of a person of another religion to preach to him and offer him Watchtower books and magazines, the Witness will not listen to anyone preach another religion and will not accept anyone else's literature. So you can not appeal to him to hear "the other side of the story." He does not want to hear the other side of the story, because he sincerely believes that it is wrong for him to listen to or even to think about anything contrary to what the Society teaches. (Even if the particular JW is one who does not really believe this, he is intimidated by the organization's system of disciplinary judicial committees and fears that he might be cut off from family and friends were he to be caught and punished for deviating from the prescribed course.)

How, then, can you share any new thoughts with someone who is so hemmed in? The most effective way is to take advantage of the JW's training to teach *you*. If he thinks he is teaching you, a Witness will discuss subjects that would have sent him fleeing if he thought that *you* were trying to teach *him*. The key to helping the individual then becomes a matter of asking the right questions.

For example, if you forcefully point out to a Jehovah's Witness that the Watchtower Society's founder, Charles Taze Russell, believed the Great Pyramid of Egypt was inspired by God, just like the Bible, and that some of Russell's false prophecies were based on his calculations of measurements of chambers within the pyramid, the Witness will view you as an opposer and will refuse to examine the documentary evidence that you offer him. But if you are the Witness's "student," and you happen to come across this material and have *questions* about it, the Witness will feel obligated to *help* you. And in the course of *helping* you he may have to look at and read the same material that he would have refused to look at if you had confronted him with it as a challenge to his faith.

Questions can thus be raised about the Watchtower Society's many false prophecies over the years, back-and-forth doctrinal changes, prohibitions on vaccinations and organ transplants that were later abandoned and other peculiar teachings not found in the Bible—beliefs that would naturally raise questions in your mind, and that should in turn cause the Jehovah's Witness himself to question whether he is really in "God's organization." If these subjects were brought up confrontationally as a challenge to his faith, the JW would become defensive and back away from examining them. But if the issues are raised unemotionally as honest questions that require answers, the Witness may find himself face-to-face with overwhelming and convincing evidence that he can not ignore.

Besides asking about these embarrassing skeletons in the Watchtower's closet, scriptural points can also be raised in the form of questions. In fact, you can even approach the JW with a list of verses that you would like some "help" with. Or, if that is not appropriate, you could present them as Scriptures that you would like to hear his comments on. The important point is to avoid any appearance of confronting the Witness, challenging him, pushing him, or otherwise trying to impose on him your understanding of the verses.

So instead of pointing at John 20:28 and saying, "See! The apostle Thomas called Jesus 'My Lord and my God!' That *proves* that Jesus is God," it would be more effective to ask the Witness to look up the verse and explain it to you. If he misses the point, use a few tactful questions to redirect his thinking. For example, he may try to minimize the import of Thomas's words by saying, "That was merely an exclamation of surprise at seeing Jesus alive again—just like you might say, 'Oh, my God!' when you are startled. Thomas didn't mean anything by it." In that case, you could ask what Jesus meant when he responded, "Have you believed because you have seen me? Blessed are those who have not seen and yet believe" (John 20:29 rsv). Ask, *What* did Thomas believe? How did his words reveal his belief? If Thomas had used the words *Lord* and *God* merely as an exclamation of surprise, wouldn't that have been blasphemy? Wouldn't Jesus have rebuked him? Why did Jesus commend him? What belief that Thomas expressed would bring blessings on others in the future who also come to believe the same thing? If I visited the local Kingdom Hall of Jehovah's Witnesses and told the elders there that I accept Jesus as "My Lord and my God," will they commend me for my belief?

The purpose of all these questions is twofold: (1) to get the JW to see what the Bible actually says, in context; and (2) to help him reach a conclusion about the meaning of the verse that is different from the prepackaged conclusion offered by his leaders.

If you *tell* him what the verse means, then you are simply offering him another prepackaged conclusion—namely, *yours*— and he must decide whether to accept yours or the Watchtower's. But, if you can skillfully ask the right questions to enable him to reach the right conclusion in his own mind, it will have a much more profound effect.

To learn how to do this—how to ask leading questions that let you *teach* answers without *telling* answers—study the example of Jesus Christ. As the greatest teacher ever to walk the earth, he knew how to instruct his hearers by asking them questions. When people doubted that he had the power to forgive sins, he asked, "Which is easier: to say to the paralytic, 'Your sins are forgiven,' or to say, 'Get up, take your mat and walk'?" (Mark 2:9 NIV). When enemies tried to trap him in the controversy over whether or not to pay taxes to Caesar, he had them produce a coin and then asked, "Whose portrait is this? And whose inscription?" (Mark 12:16 NIV) Faced with Pharisees who disapproved of his healing on the Sabbath, he asked, "Which of you, having a donkey or an ox that has fallen into a pit, will not immediately pull him out on the Sabbath day?" (Luke 14:5 NKJ). In each case the answer that his listeners were forced to come up with in their own minds was powerful and conclusive.

Besides being useful in the case of Jehovah's Witnesses, who are programmed to accept questions but not teaching from persons outside their religion, questions are a powerful teaching tool in their own right. This is because people are much more strongly impressed by answers they form in their own minds than by answers fed to them by someone else. Elementary-school-classroom teachers know and use this technique when teaching children, and you can do the same with Jehovah's Witnesses. For example, if you assert that Jesus was resurrected bodily, which is contrary to Watchtower teaching, you will make little headway with a JW; but if you have the same Witness read in John 2:19, 20 NIV: "'Destroy this temple, and I will raise it again in three days. . . .' the temple he had spoken of was *his body*," (italics added), and then ask, "What did Jesus say would happen to his body?" the Witness will *know* the right answer even if he is afraid to say it out loud.

After hearing this technique explained, a man who had previously been in the habit of arguing doctrine with his JW wife summed it up this way: Instead of wagging your finger in their faces, you get the finger to wag inside their heads.

And whose finger is it that begins to wag inside the Witness's head when Scripture is presented in this way, using questions rather than arguments? It is the finger of his or her own conscience, since deep inside, they come to realize what is right. . . . "their consciences also bearing witness, and their thoughts now accusing . . . them" (Rom. 2:15 NIV).

It is important at this point to continue to let the Holy Spirit work on the JW's thinking. Even if he cautiously begins to express some doubts about the organization, be sure not to respond too enthusiastically. Be supportive, but avoid an "I-told-you-so" response that could easily put the Witness on the defensive and abruptly halt the reeducation process.

5

Tools to Use

The principal tools that will prove useful in liberating a Jehovah's Witness fall into three main categories: (1) Scripture, (2) literature critical of the JW organization, and (3) Watchtower Society literature. In order to employ each effectively, it is necessary to understand how they can help you—or hurt your cause if used incorrectly.

Using the Bible

When using Scripture in discussions with Jehovah's Witnesses, it is important to keep in mind how they view the Bible and various translations thereof.

First of all, the organization has taught them to view the Bible as the inspired Word of God. They accept it as inerrant and authoritative. Whatever the Bible says is the final word on a subject.

Why then is it so difficult to get a Witness to see what the Bible says when it plainly refutes Watchtower doctrine? Why is it that a scriptural presentation that should reach a Witness's heart simply bounces off his chest like a BB pellet ricocheting off a Sherman tank? Why do your biblical arguments fail to penetrate the JWs thinking? The answer lies in a fuller comprehension of their view of the Bible.

Witnesses believe that the Scriptures are "the holy writings, which are able to make you wise for salvation. . . . All Scripture is inspired of God and beneficial for teaching, for reproving, for setting things straight, for disciplining in righteousness." They often quote these words from 2 Timothy 3:15, 16 (NWT), to show their reliance on the Bible, but they seldom comment on verse 17, which follows in the immediate context: "that the man of God may be fully competent, completely equipped for every good work." They may read verse 17 in order to complete the thought and to finish the sentence begun in verse 16, but in actual practice the Witnesses do not believe that the Bible alone is *sufficient* to make a person "wise for salvation." Nor is one "fully competent, completely equipped" with just the Bible. Rather it is absolutely necessary to have Watchtower Society publications that explain and interpret Scripture.

From very early in its history the organization has portrayed the Bible as worthless without Watchtower study aids to accompany it:

> . . . not only do we find that people cannot see the divine plan in studying the Bible by itself, but we see, also, that if anyone lays the SCRIPTURE STUDIES aside and goes to the Bible alone, although he has understood his Bible for ten years, our experience shows that within two years he goes into darkness. On the other hand, if he had merely read the SCRIPTURE STUDIES with their references, and had not read a page of the Bible, as such, he would be in the light at the end of the two years (*The Watch Tower*, 9/15/10, page 298).

This explains why you can not simply quote from the Bible and reach the mind and heart of a fully indoctrinated Jehovah's Witness. He or she does not dare look at the Bible alone, without the guidance of Watchtower publications. Doing so might lead to apostasy, which JWs redefine as the most deadly sin of turning away from God by rejecting "God's organization."

Speaking of some who left the organization after pursuing independent Bible study, *The Watchtower* comments:

> They say that it is sufficient to read the Bible exclusively, either alone or in small groups at home. But, strangely, through such "Bible reading," they have reverted right back to the apostate doctrines that commentaries by Christendom's clergy were teaching 100 years ago. . . (*The Watchtower*, 8/15/81, pp. 28, 29).

So if people rely on the Bible alone, without Watchtower Society study guides, they tend to return to the doctrines of traditional Christianity. What a strange admission! Still, not realizing the irony of such a statement, Jehovah's Witnesses get the point that they must never read Scripture without subjecting it to the organization's interpretation. In effect, they look at the Bible through Watchtower-tinted lenses. They see in the Word only what they are told to see.

If you yourself have never been a Witness, this may be difficult to grasp. It is hard to understand how someone can see a clear statement in the Bible, read it out loud, repeat it from memory, and still not get the point of what the verse is saying. But the encounter, mentioned earlier, that I had with two JW ladies on my own doorstep well illustrated that this is exactly what happens. Remember in Chapter 3 I had asked one of them to read Revelation 19:1, in her own Bible, to see where it positions the "great crowd"? She obligingly opened her *New World Translation* and read, "'After these things I heard what was as a loud voice of a great crowd in heaven.'" "The 'great crowd' is on earth!", she commented, eventually admitting that, "It *says heaven*, but the 'great crowd' is on *earth*," because, "We have men at our headquarters in Brooklyn, New York, who explain the Bible to us. And they can prove that the 'great crowd' is on earth; I just can't explain it that well."

So although the Witnesses will tote their Bibles to your door and will read from Scripture to support their teachings, they are not actually taking their instruction from the Word of God, but rather from the men at Watchtower headquarters who tell them what the Bible says and what it means. Likewise, when you show them a verse, have them read it, and ask them what it says, their response is governed by the prior indoctrination they have received, rather than by what they have just read from the page.

To cope with this type of behavior on the part of the particular Witness you are trying to help, you must remember that what is happening is more than what meets the eye. When you ask the individual to read a verse from the Bible, he or she reads it—and then instantaneously does something else without your knowledge. The person's preprogrammed mind automatically replaces what the verse says with the organization's interpretation of what it says. This is not a conscious dodge, but rather a knee-jerk, reflex action that the JW is not even aware of. Reading the verse triggers the official interpretation to pop up in the brain.

Being aware that this is what goes on in the Witness's mind, you are in a better position to handle a biblical discussion. You will realize that it is not enough simply to read a verse and comment on it. Painstaking effort is necessary in order to get the JW to truly grasp what the verse says. The following steps are often helpful.

1. Rather than read the verse yourself, ask the Witness to read it aloud from the organization's *New World Translation*. (If you simply quote the verse from memory, the JW may assume that you misquoted it; or, if you read it first from a non-Witness translation, that it was mistranslated.)

2. Have the Witness break down the verse into clauses, phrases, and individual words. Ask him or her to comment on what each means. The Watchtower interpretation of the whole may disintegrate when the parts are examined separately.

3. Read the same verse from other translations: first from the Watchtower Society's *Kingdom Interlinear* word-for-word rendering of the Greek, then perhaps from Samuel T. Byington's *The Bible in Living English* (also published by the Watchtower Society), and finally from a few other recognized translations—a multiversion parallel Bible is helpful in this and can be obtained through a local Christian bookstore. Unless you are considering one of the few hundred verses that Watchtower translators altered to fit official doctrine, the purpose of such a comparison would not be to discredit the *New World Translation* but rather to avoid the word pattern that triggers recall of the preprogrammed interpretation.

For example, while reading the NWT's familiar wording of Christ's command regarding the communion cup, to "Drink out of it, all of you," the Witness likely will see no contradiction in the Watchtower's teaching that only a small percentage of believers should partake. But reading *"Each one* drink from it" in *The Living Bible's* paraphrase might be just enough to get him to see that "all of you" in the NWT really means *"all* of you"! (Matt. 26:27, italics added).

Before leaving the subject of how to use the Bible, a word

about the *New World Translation* itself is in order. For a number
of years Jehovah's Witnesses carried with them to their neighbors' doors a green-covered copy of this Bible. The green cover
was helpful as a warning to non-Witnesses, because it tipped
them off that something was different. More recently, however,
the Brooklyn Bethel factories have been turning out NWT's with
black covers, making them easier to pass off as ordinary Bibles.
But that could not be further from the truth. Actually, the *New
World Translation* contains hundreds of verses that have been
altered to fit Watchtower doctrine.

Before it was published, Witnesses had to employ the standard translations used by everyone else. Their printing presses
actually produced thousands of copies of the King James Version. Then they began using the American Standard Version,
because it featured the name *Jehovah* more frequently in the
Old Testament. But JWs were constantly facing the embarrassing problem of a knowledgeable householder asking them to
look up John 1:1, where Jesus Christ is identified as "God," or
Galatians 6:14, where it speaks of "the cross of our Lord Jesus
Christ." Now, with their own tailor-made version, they can
turn to these same verses and show that Jesus is merely "a god,"
and that he was put to death on a "torture stake" instead of a
cross.

There is much more that could be said about the NWT; in fact,
whole books have been written about it. But the important point
to bear in mind when having discussions with a JW loved one is
this: while it may prove useful to show the Witness that a
certain point is in fact in *his* Bible, the NWT should not be relied
on for unbiased accurate renderings of the Word of God.

Using Other Books

In addition to this book there are many others written by
Christians to expose the errors of the Watchtower Society (*see*
Appendix). For instance, as mentioned before there is my own
Jehovah's Witnesses Answered Verse by Verse, a quick refer-
ence guide that discusses dozens of passages misinterpreted by
JWs and suggests how to respond to them in each case. The more
such aids you read before your encounter, the better. They can

make you more familiar with the sect's history and beliefs, and can prepare you for some of the off-the-wall arguments you can expect from well-trained JWs.

But these books are best left unseen and preferably unmentioned to the Witness. The only book that you should bring to the table is the Bible itself, with the possible exception of Watchtower literature, which we will discuss shortly. (Your own hand-written notes are best kept on a small sheet of paper taped inside your Bible.)

The reason that other literature should be kept out of sight is twofold: (1) Having on hand material written by an apostate ex-Witness like myself would be almost as offensive as having a disfellowshiped person join you at the table. The JW views "reading apostate publications [as] similar to reading pornographic literature" (*The Watchtower*, 3/15/86, p. 14). If he knows that you are using such materials, he will suspect that you may be a willing instrument of the devil, or else duped by "wicked apostates." On one occasion back in the days when I was a JW elder, I took the traveling Circuit Overseer with me to visit a man who had expressed an interest in talking with us. We had just stepped inside and had exchanged no more than a greeting with the man, when my companion noticed some anti-Witness books on the table. "Come on, Dave! Let's get out of here!" he barked, turning toward the door. "We're not supposed to cast our pearls before swine!" Your discussion with a Witness could similarly be cut short if a book such as the one you are now holding were to be seen. (2) It should be made clear that your faith and your beliefs are based on the Bible alone, rather than books authored by men. This should stand out in sharp contrast to the Witness, who depends completely on publications of the Watchtower Bible and Tract Society. If he sees you using books in addition to the Bible, he will automatically assume that you derive your beliefs from your books, the same as he does his.

Using Watchtower Literature

The most powerful tool you can use to help a fully indoctrinated Jehovah's Witness is *his own literature*. But, how could that be so? Would not his own literature simply reinforce his existing beliefs? No, because it is here that you will find the documentary evidence disproving the Watchtower Society's claim to divine authority.

Buried in the back issues of *The Watchtower* are countless contradictions, false prophecies, back-and-forth doctrinal changes, fraudulent deceptions, and patently ludicrous notions—all taught as "the Truth." As we shall see in later chapters, the leaders in Brooklyn at one time believed that the Great Pyramid of Egypt contained prophetic wisdom from God; later, they decided the Pyramid was Satan's Bible. Although condemning others as false prophets, they themselves predicted that the world would end in 1914; later, that the patriarchs Abraham, Isaac, and Jacob would rise from the grave in 1925; and, more recently, that the world would end and the thousand-year-reign of Christ would begin in 1975. For years they taught that Almighty God Jehovah resided in a particular location in outer space, namely, on the star Alcyone in the Pleiades star system. They proclaimed that God forbade certain medical procedures, allowed their followers to suffer or die in obedience to these beliefs, and then years later dropped the prohibitions.

Most Jehovah's Witnesses have no idea that these things happened; or else, they have heard a vague, sugar-coated version. For example, they often hear in their Kingdom Halls that the Watchtower Society back in the 1800s predicted a world war for 1914, the year World War I broke out; whereas the war predicted for that year was actually the Battle of Armageddon, in which God would destroy all human governments, replacing them with his kingdom. When confronted with the facts on such matters, JWs can not help but be shocked. And presented with one such shock after another, they can not help but question their leaders' claim to speak for God.

The evidence is all right there, in black and white, in the pages of the Society's publications. Although instructed not to read other people's "false religious literature that is designed to deceive" (*The Watchtower*, 5/1/84, p. 31), Witnesses can hardly refuse to look at *their own* literature. In fact, each one collects a personal library of the organization's books for that very purpose, and they are accustomed to doing research and looking up information in back issues of their magazines.

But it usually is not sufficient merely to quote the literature, citing the publication, page, and paragraph. The Witness will likely assume you misquoted it, or will favorably alter the quote in his own mind and never bother to look it up for verification. The most effective approach is to produce a photocopy of the actual page, with the quote highlighted, circled or underlined in its original context. This can not be dismissed as a baseless, hostile accusation. In fact, it is not your accusation that the Witness must contend with, but rather the Watchtower Society's own words printed in its own publications—literature that the JW has been taught to revere as coming from "God's organization." Jesus said, ". . . out of your own mouth you will be condemned" (Matt. 12:37 NEB), and the Watchtower leadership certainly has furnished more than enough evidence out of its own mouth to condemn it before God and man.

Even here you must exercise discernment as to when and how you will share these photocopies with a particular Jehovah's Witness. Since the originals are not available to you and you are copying from a book such as ours, be sure to block out or cut off any added headings or page numbers, so that only the original Watchtower headings and page numbers remain. And then present them as "copies of Watchtower literature," which they truly are, rather than mentioning that you got them secondhand from another book. Be sure to read the highlighted quotes aloud with the Witness, rather than just hand him or her a pile of papers in the hope that he or she will read them later on. But let the quotes themselves do most of the talking, rather than your repeatedly hammering home the point that the organization is false. After reading all the quotes in a calm, prayerful atmosphere, the JW will reach that conclusion himself, whether or not he admits it to you then.

Literature to Give the JW to Read

As pointed out above, anti-Witness literature is best kept hidden from sight and unmentioned during discussions with JWs. Eventually, however, if those discussions prove successful, the Witness will want to start reading some outside material to further explore the organization's errors on his own. What should you recommend or give him to read? It should be something written especially for Witnesses, preferably by a former member who understands how they think. Most anti-Witness literature is written by Christians *for* Christians, not for JWs themselves to read. Such books employ certain basic assumptions and vocabulary peculiar to churched people that a Jehovah's Witness reader would find either confusing or offensive or both.

Of the few books written for JWs by ex-JWs, the one that has shown itself most effective in helping them decide to leave the sect is *Crisis of Conscience* by Raymond V. Franz. This is the personal story of a man who spent most of his life in full-time Watchtower service, including nine years as a member of the elite Governing Body in Brooklyn, the group's supreme council. Nephew of President Frederick W. Franz, Raymond personally wrote Watchtower literature and shared in deciding what would be taught as the revealed "truth"—until his conscience finally got the best of him and he found himself in conflict with his peers, resulting in his expulsion. Although "boring" to many non-Witness readers, *Crisis of Conscience* is so fascinating to JWs that many will read it in spite of the knowledge that they could be put on trial and punished if caught with the book in their possession. And those who do read it usually leave the organization as a result. If not available through a local Christian book store, Franz's book can be ordered direct from the publisher or through Comments from the Friends, P.O. Box 840, Stoughton, MA 02072.

6

Step-by-Step

If you have read and digested the preceding chapters, you are now ready to consider specific material to present to your Jehovah's Witness loved one. Ideally this should be done step-by-step over a period of time. It takes time to program a person into a cultic mentality; so, likewise, it takes time to deprogram. Rushing the process can result in an aborted attempt—something that can not be risked when there may not be opportunity for a second attempt.

The material assembled here will have a powerful impact on a Jehovah's Witness. No JW can read these selections and simply shrug. Rather he or she will find them extremely unsettling, giving rise to strong emotions and intense reevaluation of beliefs.

However, you should not expect to see an immediate outward manifestation of this. Jehovah's Witnesses have been trained to keep their real feelings to themselves, especially doubts, fears, and insecurities about their beliefs. To express open disbelief in Watchtower teachings is to expose oneself to censure and possible expulsion, so JWs learn to mask their inward questionings and to hide their secret thoughts even from their most intimate associates.

For example, consider the situation that developed among my in-laws. My wife's parents began to study with the Witnesses while Penni was in elementary school, and soon became dedicated, baptized JWs. So they had been in the organization for a good portion of their lives when Penni and I, in the eleventh year of our marriage, agreed to quit the sect. We visited her parents to tell them of our decision, knowing that the reaction they had been programmed to give would be to throw us out of the house and refuse to see us anymore. You can imagine our surprise then to discover that they themselves had wanted to leave the organization for a long time, but had held back from doing so because Penni and I were so firmly entrenched in it that they expected *we* would cut *them* off. They hid from us their true feelings throughout all that time. So as the evidence you share with your Witness friend begins to weigh more and more heavily on his heart, do not expect him to tell you so. In most cases he will be unable to discuss the direction in which his thoughts are moving until he has reached an irrevocable decision to break with the organization. Any disclosure before that could result in his being forcibly expelled before he is ready to leave.

However it should also be noted that the Witness exposed to the information we are about to present may react in one of two opposite ways: he may flee from the Watchtower organization and seek out true Christianity, or he may flee to the security of the Kingdom Hall and resolve never again to critically examine his religion.

I have seen both reactions in different individuals. Consider "Karen," for example. A minister she met in her door-to-door canvassing shared with her some information that shook her faith in the Brooklyn leadership. She spent a couple of days in emotional turmoil, seeking help from "spiritually mature" persons in the congregation. But she ended up settling the matter by sticking her head deeper in the sand. In the future she would be quicker to walk away from anyone presenting apostate ideas—she wanted never to face that sort of mental anguish again.

Whether a given individual will be liberated or further enslaved by an encounter with the truth will depend on a number of factors, some of which you can not influence (for example, his or her personality, family circumstances, and so forth) and some of which you *can* control (for instance, your timing, approach, techniques, personal example, and so forth). Since the factors within your control may be enough to tip the balance one way or the other, it is imperative that you give due attention to the thoughts in our previous chapters on strategy, timing, techniques, and approach, as well as the remaining chapters of this book. Applying these suggestions may mean the difference between success and failure. Moreover, since a bungled attempt may bar you from the opportunity to try again, you should muster all available resources to do it right the first time.

Rather than dispute various Jehovah's Witness beliefs one at a time, we have seen that the most effective strategy is one that takes aim at the Watchtower organization itself—the very basis for all of those false beliefs. "Is the Watchtower organization truly what it claims to be?" That should be the focus of early discussions with a JW, until the Witness sees the organization for what it really is. After that, and only after that, can you successfully challenge the doctrinal beliefs that are now left to stand on their own without being upheld by the Watchtower's authority. If the organization is what it claims to be, then all of its teachings *must* be true. But if it is an impostor, then all of its teachings are suspect.

In brief, these are the steps you will need to take:

1. *Establish the Watchtower Society's claims.* As a defensive maneuver, JWs will sometimes insist to outsiders that their leaders are "just ordinary people like us, who study the Bible and try their best to teach what it says." To head off this defense, you must first document that the organization claims to be God's prophet and the exclusive channel of communication that God is using.

2. *Disprove the organization's claims.* Since it claims to be a prophet, examine its prophecies to demonstrate that it is indeed a *false* prophet. Since it claims to be the channel of communication from God, examine some of the ideas it has communicated that could not possibly have originated with God.

3. *Draw the conclusion that the Watchtower is not God's organization.* At this point the Witness's sense of obligation to the sect ends, and he or she is free to rethink beliefs and redirect life's goals and ambitions.

4. *Establish the real truth.* Help the JW fill the void left by the Watchtower by getting to know God and coming into fellowship with genuine Christians.

5. *Aid in deprogramming and readjustment.* It takes years for a fully indoctrinated Jehovah's Witness to shed all the mental

and emotional encumbrances acquired while in the sect. The resources and ex-member support groups listed at the end of this book will prove helpful in this.

The next few chapters enable you first to establish the claims the Watchtower's leaders have made for themselves and then to demonstrate the falsehood of those claims. To aid you in accomplishing this we provide documentation of the organization's statements, along with suggestions for discussing these with your Jehovah's Witness loved one. Bearing in mind that Witnesses are forbidden to read apostate literature, it would be unwise to show them this book. Not only would they normally refuse to look at it, but they might also feel obliged to cease discussions with you since you are passing on to them so-called apostate ideas. Instead, photocopy the documents individually and present them as pages from Watchtower publications— which they truly are, and which Witnesses should feel free to read. (Note: Page numbers in brackets following name, date, page number of the publication quoted refer to the page number at the end of the chapter, where photocopies of the original publications can be found. The quotes are indicated by ⌐ ¬ for easier location by the reader.)

7

God's "Prophet"

Typically, the Watchtower Society promotes itself as God's prophet by the very act of prophesying. But on a few occasions it has even come right out and ascribed to itself the title "prophet." Before presenting the material on the sect's false prophecies, you will need to be sure that the Jehovah's Witness understands that the organization actually does identify itself as God's "prophet." This is because the organization also asserts that it is *not* a prophet.

Isn't that a contradiction? Yes, but it is typical of cultic reasoning. In this connection, the Witnesses have learned to practice *double-think*, the mental gymnastics described in George Orwell's novel *Nineteen Eighty-Four*, where people are forced by a totalitarian state, ". . . To know and not to know, to be conscious of complete truthfulness while telling carefully constructed lies, to hold simultaneously two opinions which canceled out, knowing them to be contradictory and believing in both of them . . ." (*Nineteen Eighty-Four* New American Library, 1981, p. 32).

Double-think enables Witnesses to believe with all their heart that the Society is God's prophet, and yet when confronted with the charge of "false prophesying" to deny that the organization ever claimed to be a prophet. Thus in a discussion aimed at teaching JWs how to defend themselves "If someone says—'My minister said that Jehovah's Witnesses are the false prophets,'" the Watchtower book *Reasoning from the Scriptures* offers the answer, "Jehovah's Witnesses do not claim to be inspired prophets" (1985, pp. 136, 137).

Yet, during the late 1970s and throughout 1980, each issue of their principal magazine featured this assertion as part of its masthead: "A WATCHTOWER enables a person to look far into the distance and announce to others what is seen. Likewise, this magazine, published by Jehovah's Witnesses, aids the reader to see what the future holds" (*The Watchtower*, 1/1/80, p. 2). By definition, one who tells what the future holds is, of course, a prophet.

A few years earlier a similar statement regularly appeared in the masthead, but it was qualified like this:

> "Ever since 'The Watchtower' began to be published in July of 1879 it has looked ahead into the future . . . No, 'The Watchtower' is no inspired prophet, but it follows and explains a Book of prophecy the predictions in which have proved to be unerring and unfailing till now. 'The Watchtower' is therefore under safe guidance. It may be read with confidence, for its statements may be checked against that prophetic Book" (*The Watchtower*, 1/1/69, p. 2).

So, a fine line of distinction is drawn: the magazine is not an inspired prophet, but it merely explains prophecies found in the Bible. However, those "explanations" often go far beyond what the Bible says, even to the point of naming specific dates such as 1914, 1918, 1925, and 1975, as we shall see below. When someone "explaining" the Bible begins to predict what will happen on certain dates in the future—dates mentioned nowhere in Scripture—he can no longer claim that it is the Bible that is speaking; he is now acting as a prophet in his own right.

To establish with your Jehovah's Witness friend the fact that the organization has indeed called itself a "prophet," read with him these statements from *The Watchtower* (4/1/72, p. 197) found in an article titled "'They shall know that a prophet was among them'":

> People today can view the creative works. They have at hand the Bible, but it is little read or understood. So, does Jehovah have a prophet to help them, to warn them of dangers and to declare things to come? . . . These questions can be answered in the

affirmative. Who is this prophet? . . . This "prophet" was not one man, but was a body of men and women. It was the small group of footstep followers of Jesus Christ, known at that time as International Bible Students. Today they are known as Jehovah's Witnesses. . . . Of course, it is easy to say that this group acts as a "prophet" of God. It is another thing to prove it. The only way that this can be done is to review the record [see p. 61].

Tell the Witness that you accept *The Watchtower's* invitation to "review the record," and that you have researched the matter and collected some photocopies that document the record the organization has made for itself as a prophet. (As mentioned earlier, it would be best to show the Witness photocopies you have made, rather than show him this "apostate" book.) Before getting into the specifics, invite him to turn in his own Bible to Deuteronomy 18:20-22, to see what God's Word says about true and false prophets. The true ones are highly esteemed as men of God, but false ones are judged to be worthy of death:

> However, the prophet who presumes to speak in my name a word that I have not commanded him to speak or who speaks in the name of other gods, that prophet must die. And in case you should say in your heart: "How shall we know the word that Jehovah has spoken?" when the prophet speaks in the name of Jehovah and the word does not occur or come true, that is the word that Jehovah did not speak. With presumptuousness the prophet spoke it. . . (NWT).

So, God himself has established the criteria for judging true and false prophets: (1) Is the utterance spoken in his name or in the name of other gods; and (2) does the word spoken occur or come true? Now it is simply a matter of comparing the Watchtower prophecies to this divinely inspired standard of judgment. Obviously the Jehovah's Witness organization has spoken in the name of Jehovah, so it is okay on point number one. But have the messages spoken occurred or come true? If not, then the condemnation of God is on the organization and it is worthy of death, because it has presumptuously pretended to speak for God.

In the case of ancient Israel, where the standard of Deuteronomy 18:20-22 was first applied, prophets usually communicated their pronouncements by means of the spoken word. At times they addressed kings in private, and at other times, large gatherings of people in public places. In order to determine whether what was prophesied actually occurred or came true, hearers would have to testify as to what they had heard the prophet speak. But in the case of the Watchtower Society, most of its prophetic statements have been made in the pages of its books and magazines. Thus, they are preserved in black and white, and it becomes a simple matter of comparing what was said with what actually occurred.

For example, the Watchtower Society prophesied during the late 1800s and early 1900s that God would wage his final war of Armageddon in the year 1914, destroying all human governments and replacing them with the rulership of the kingdom of God over all the earth by the end of that year:

> True, it is expecting great things to claim, as we do, that within the coming twenty-six years all present governments will be overthrown and dissolved . . . In view of this strong Bible evidence concerning the Times of the Gentiles, we consider it an established truth that the final end of the kingdoms of this world, and the full establishment of the Kingdom of God, will be accomplished at the end of A. D. 1914. . . . (*The Time is at Hand* [*Studies in the Scriptures*, vol. II], Watch Tower Bible and Tract Society, 1889 [1908 edition], pp. 98, 99 [*see* pp. 62–64]).

This prophecy that God would intervene to end the world of wicked mankind in 1914 was repeated many times in Watchtower publications, until 1914 came and went, proving the prophecy false.

In 1917, the Society predicted that the churches would soon "cease to be" because God would destroy them in the following year, 1918, with any survivors forced to become readers of the books of C. T. Russell, the Watchtower's first president:

> . . . Also, in the year 1918, when God destroys the churches wholesale and the church members by millions, it shall be that any that escape shall come to the works of Pastor Russell to learn the meaning of the downfall of "Christianity" (*The Finished Mystery* [*Studies in the Scriptures*, vol. VII], 1917 [1917 edition], p. 485 [*see* pp. 65–66]).

In 1920 Watchtower representatives worldwide delivered a special lecture titled "Millions Now Living Will Never Die," and a book by the Society's second president, J. F. Rutherford, was circulated, in which the organization prophesied that many Old Testament Bible characters would be raised to life in 1925:

> . . . They are to be resurrected as perfect men and constitute the princes or rulers in the earth. . . . Therefore we may confidently expect that 1925 will mark the return of Abraham, Isaac, Jacob and the faithful prophets of old. . . . 1925 shall mark the resurrection of the faithful worthies of old and the beginning of reconstruction. . . (J. F. Rutherford, *Millions Now Living Will Never Die*, 1920, pp. 89, 90, 97 [*see* pp. 67–69]).

During the mid-1960s Jehovah's Witnesses began to hear remarks from their leaders pointing forward to the year 1975 as the date for the end of this old world and the beginning of Christ's millennial reign:

> . . . According to this trustworthy Bible chronology six thousand years from man's creation will end in 1975, and the seventh period of a thousand years of human history will begin in the fall of 1975 C.E. . . . It would not be by mere chance or accident but would be according to the loving purpose of Jehovah God for the reign of Jesus Christ, the "Lord of the Sabbath," to run parallel with the seventh millenium of man's existence (*Life Everlasting—in Freedom of the Sons of God*, 1966, pp. 29, 30 [*see* pp. 70–71]).

During the next few years the organization made many more references to 1975, perhaps the most detailed being in an August 15, 1968, *Watchtower* article titled "Why Are You Looking Forward to 1975?" (p. 494 [*see* p. 72]). In this article the Society stated:

> Are we to assume from this study that the battle of Armageddon will be all over by the autumn of 1975, and the long-looked-for thousand-year reign of Christ will begin by then? Possibly, but we wait to see how closely the seventh thousand-year period of man's existence coincides with the sabbathlike thousand-year reign of Christ. . . . It may involve only a difference of weeks or months, not years (*The Watchtower*, 8/15/68, p. 499 [*see* p. 73]).

How could Jehovah's Witnesses back then demonstrate that they did not view the Society's prophecy about 1975 as mere academic speculation, but actually accepted it as truth to live by? Their monthly publication *Kingdom Ministry* suggested that they quit their jobs, sell their homes, and live off that money in order to be full-time ("pioneer") Watchtower distributors during the short time remaining before "the end":

> Yes, the end of this system is so very near! Is this not reason to increase our activity? . . . Reports are heard of brothers selling their homes and property and planning to finish out the rest of their days in this old system in the pioneer service. Certainly this is a fine way to spend the short time remaining before the wicked world's end. . . (*Kingdom Ministry*, May 1974, p. 3 [see p. 74]).

Having already served some years in "pioneer" work, I had no home or property to sell. But I did neglect having necessary dental work done, figuring it would be better to devote my time and funds to "spiritual things," since the end was so near and my body would be restored to perfection shortly after 1975.

The things prophesied to take place in 1914, 1918, 1925, and 1975 did not happen, of course, so the Watchtower Society has proved to be a false prophet many times over. This should be discussed as dispassionately as possible. Let the Witness grasp the point without trying to hammer it in with an *I-told-you-so!* remark that would only get in the way of his admitting the facts. A better approach might be to conclude the discussion with a rereading of Deuteronomy 18:20-22, quoted above, perhaps adding also Jesus' words at Matthew 7:15, "Beware of false prophets, which come to you in sheep's clothing, but inwardly they are ravening wolves"(KJV).

Still, rather than put your JW loved one on the spot by demanding an immediate acknowledgment that the Watchtower Society is one of those wolves in sheep's clothing, it would be better to let the facts speak for themselves. This will make it more tolerable for the Witness to continue listening as you present the material in the next few chapters.

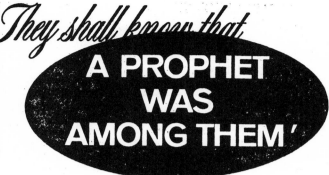

A PROPHET
WAS
AMONG THEM'

JEHOVAH GOD is interested in having people know him. Though he is invisible to human eyes, he provides various ways by which they can know his personality. They can know what to expect from him and what he expects of them.

One can come to understand that Jehovah is a God of surpassing wisdom by observing creation. This also reveals the loving care with which he designed things for man's welfare and enjoyment. A second way to know God is through his Word of truth, the Bible. Herein one finds the full expression of Jehovah's purpose toward mankind—why man is on the earth and the blessings that God has in store.

A third way of coming to know Jehovah God is through his representatives. In ancient times he sent prophets as his special messengers. While these men foretold things to come, they also served the people by telling them of God's will for them at that time, often also warning them of dangers and calamities. People today can view the creative works. They have at hand the Bible, but it is little read or understood. So, does Jehovah have a prophet to help them, to warn them of dangers and to declare things to come?

IDENTIFYING THE "PROPHET"

These questions can be answered in the affirmative. Who is this prophet? The cler-

gy of the so-called "Christian" nations hold themselves before the people as being the ones commissioned to speak for God. But, as pointed out in the previous issue of this magazine, they have failed God and failed as proclaimers of his kingdom by approving a man-made political organization, the League of Nations (now the United Nations), as "the political expression of the Kingdom of God on earth."

However, Jehovah did not let the people of Christendom, as led by the clergy, go without being warned that the League was a counterfeit substitute for the real kingdom of God. He had a "prophet" to warn them. This "prophet" was not one man, but was a body of men and women. It was the small group of footstep followers of Jesus Christ, known at that time as International Bible Students. Today they are known as Jehovah's Christian witnesses. They are still proclaiming a warning, and have been joined and assisted in their commissioned work by hundreds of thousands of persons who have listened to their message with belief.

Of course, it is easy to say that this group acts as a "prophet" of God. It is another thing to prove it. The only way that this can be done is to review the record. What does it show?

During the World War I period this group, the International Bible Students, was very active in preaching the good news of God's kingdom, as their Leader Jesus Christ had set this work before them in his prophecy at Matthew 24:14. They took literally Jesus' words to the Roman governor Pontius Pilate: "My kingdom is no part of this world." (John 18:36) They also took to heart Jesus' words to his fol-

STUDIES

—IN THE—

SCRIPTURES

"THE PATH OF THE JUST IS AS THE SHINING LIGHT, WHICH SHINETH MORE
AND MORE UNTO THE PERFECT DAY."

SERIES II.

The Time is at Hand.

627,000 Edition

"TIMES OF REFRESHING SHALL COME FROM THE PRESENCE OF THE LORD : AND
HE SHALL SEND JESUS CHRIST, * * * WHOM THE
HEAVENS MUST RETAIN UNTIL

THE TIMES OF RESTITUTION OF ALL THINGS,

WHICH GOD HATH SPOKEN BY THE MOUTH OF ALL HIS HOLY PROPHETS SINCE THE
WORLD BEGAN." "YE, BRETHREN, ARE NOT IN DARKNESS, THAT THAT
DAY SHOULD OVERTAKE YOU AS A THIEF."
ACTS 3 : 19–21 ; I THES. 5 : 4.

WATCH TOWER
BIBLE AND TRACT SOCIETY,
ALLEGHENY, PA., U. S. A.

1908

The Time is at Hand, 1908 edition, title page

How refreshing the prospect brought to view at the close of these seven times! Neither Israel nor the world of mankind represented by that people will longer be trodden down, oppressed and misruled by beastly Gentile powers. The Kingdom of God and his Christ will then be established in the earth, and Israel and all the world will be blessed under his rightful and righteous authority. Then the root of promise and hope planted first in Eden (Gen. 3: 15), and borne across the flood and transplanted with Israel the typical people (Gen. 12: 1–3), will sprout and bloom again.

It began to sprout at our Lord's first advent, but the appointed season had not arrived for it to bloom and bring forth its blessed fruitage in the restitution of all things. But at the end of the Gentile Times the sure signs of spring will not be lacking, and rich will be the summer fruitage and glorious the autumnal harvest to be reaped and enjoyed in the eternal ages of glory to follow. Then the original lord of earth, with reason restored, will be fully re-instated, with added excellence and glory, as in the type, and will praise and extol and honor the King of heaven.

Already we begin to see reason returning to mankind: men are awakening to some sense of their degradation, and are on the lookout to improve their condition. They are thinking, planning and scheming for a better condition than that to which they have been submitting under the beastly powers. But before they come to recognize God and his dominion over all, they will experience one more terrible fit of madness, from which struggle they will awake weak, helpless, exhausted, but with reason so far restored as to recognize and bow to the authority of him who comes to re-establish the long lost, first dominion, on the permanent basis of experience and knowledge of both good and evil.

True, it is expecting great things to claim, as we do, that within the coming twenty-six years all present governments

The Time is at Hand, 1908 edition, p. 98

Times of the Gentiles.   **99**

will be overthrown and dissolved ? but we are living in a special and peculiar time, the " Day of Jehovah," in which matters culminate quickly ; and it is written, " A short work will the Lord make upon the earth." (See Vol. I., chap. xv.) For the past eleven years these things have been preached and published substantially as set forth above ; and in that brief time the development of influences and agencies for the undermining and overthrow of the strongest empires of earth has been wonderful. In that time Communism, Socialism and Nihilism sprang into vigorous existence, and already are causing great uneasiness among the rulers and high ones of earth, whose hearts are failing them for fear, and for looking after those things which are coming on the earth ; for the present powers are being mightily shaken, and ultimately shall pass away with a great tumult.

ᒷIn view of this strong Bible evidence concerning the Times of the Gentiles, we consider it an established truth that the final end of the kingdoms of this world, and the full establishment of the Kingdom of God, will be accomplished at the end of A. D. 1914ᒣ Then the prayer of the Church, ever since her Lord took his departure—" Thy Kingdom come"—will be answered ; and under that wise and just administration, the whole earth will be filled with the glory of the Lord—with knowledge, and righteousness, and peace (Psa. 72 : 19 ; Isa. 6 : 3 ; Hab. 2 : 14) ; and the will of God shall be done *"on earth, as it is done in heaven."*

Daniel's statement, that God's Kingdom will be set up, not after these kingdoms of earth are dissolved, but in their days, while they still exist and have power, and that it is God's Kingdom which shall break in pieces and consume all these kingdoms (Dan. 2 : 44), is worthy of our special consideration. So it was with each of these beastly governments : it existed before it acquired universal dominion. Babylon existed long before it conquered Jerusalem and

The Time is at Hand, 1908 edition, p. 99

24:18. So I spake unto the people in the morning: and at even my wife died; and I did in the morning as I was commanded.—He continued his addresses and writings to the Lord's people; his wife became to him as one dead; and he continued uninterruptedly in the work of the ministry.

24:19. And the people said unto me, Wilt thou not tell us what these things are to us, that thou doest so?—Why was Pastor Russell caused by his Father to endure the fiery trials and ecclesiastical falsehoods in connection with this incident of his life?

⌈THE CHURCHES TO CEASE TO BE⌉

24:20, 21. Then I answered them, The word of the Lord came unto me, saying, Speak unto the house of Israel, Thus saith the Lord God; Behold, I will profane My Sanctuary, the excellency of your strength, the desire of your eyes, and that which your soul pitieth; and your sons and your daughters whom ye have left shall fall by the sword.—God gives the reason. It was as a picture or parable of what is to happen to Christendom. Until 1878 the nominal church had been in a sense God's sanctuary or Temple; but He was from then on, culminating in 1918, to remove it with a stroke or plague of erroneous doctrines and deeds Divinely permitted. The Church was the strength of Christendom, that about which its life centered, and around which its institutions were built. It was the desire of the eyes of the people, that which all Christians loved. Nevertheless, God was to make manifest the profanation which ecclesiasticism had made of the Christian Church, and to cause the church organizations to become to Him as one dead, an unclean thing, not to be touched, or mourned. And the "children of the church" shall perish by the sword of war, revolution and anarchy, and by the Sword of the Spirit be made to see that they have lost their hope of life on the spirit plane—that "the door is shut."

24:22. And ye shall do as I have done: ye shall not cover your lips, nor eat the bread of men.—So universal and dreadful will be the troubles that the dead will literally lie unburied and unwept. There can be no mourning for the dead in a period when the living are overwhelmed by troubles worse than death.

24:23. And your tires shall be upon your heads; and your shoes upon your feet: ye shall not mourn nor weep; but ye shall pine away for your iniquities, and mourn one toward another.—The mourning will be an inner sorrow of a people stupefied by terrible experiences, who pine

The Boiling Caldron   **485**

away and without outward expression sink together into
the fellowship of helpless grief.

**24:24. Thus Ezekiel is unto you a sign: according to all
that he hath done shall ye do: and when this cometh, ye
shall know that I am the Lord God.**—Thus the silent sorrow at Pastor Russell's heart was to be a sign to Christendom. The sorrowful experiences of Pastor Russell in this
connection shall later on be those of all Christendom;
"and when this cometh" they shall know that Jehovah God
is supreme, and back of all the judgments of the trouble
time.

PASTOR RUSSELL DEAD, BUT SPEAKING AGAIN

**24:25, 26. Also, thou son of man, shall it not be in the
day when I take from them their strength, the joy
of their glory, the desire of their eyes, and that whereupon
they set their minds, their sons and their daughters. That
he that escapeth in that day shall come unto thee, to cause
thee to hear it with thine ears?**—Also, in the year 1918,
when God destroys the churches wholesale and the church
members by millions, it shall be that any that escape shall
come to the works of Pastor Russell to learn the meaning
of the downfall of "Christianity."[7]

**24:27. In that day shall thy mouth be opened to him
which is escaped, and thou shalt speak, and be no more
dumb: and thou shalt be a sign unto them; and they shall
know that I am the Lord.**—Pastor Russell's voice has been
stilled in death; and his voice is, comparatively speaking,
dumb to what it will be. In the time of revolution and
anarchy he shall speak, and be no more dumb to those
that escape the destruction of that day. Pastor Russell
shall "be a sign unto them," shall tell them the truth about
the Divine appointment of the trouble, as they consult his
books, scattered to the number of ten million throughout Christendom. His words shall be a sign of hope unto
them, enabling them to see the bright side of the cloud
and to look forward with anticipation to the glorious
Kingdom of God to be established. Then "they shall know
the Lord."

" Build thee more stately mansions, O my soul,
    As the swift seasons roll!
    Leave thy low vaulted past!
Let each new temple, nobler than the last,
Shut thee from heaven with a dome more vast,
    Till thou at length art free,
Leaving thine outgrown shell by life's unresting sea."

The Finished Mystery, 1917 edition, p. 485

the hills; and people shall flow unto it. And many nations shall come, and say, Come, and let us go up to the mountain of the Lord, and to the house of the God of Jacob; and he will teach us of his ways, and we will walk in his paths: for the law shall go forth of Zion, and the word *of the Lord from Jerusalem. And he shall judge* among many people, and rebuke strong nations afar off; and they shall beat their swords into plowshares, and their spears into pruninghooks; nation shall not life up a sword against nation, neither shall they learn war any more. But they shall sit every man under his vine and under his fig tree; and none shall make them afraid; for the mouth of the Lord of hosts hath spoken it." —Micah 4: 1 - 4.

EARTHLY RULERS

As we have heretofore stated, the great jubilee cycle is due to begin in 1925. At that time the earthly phase of the kingdom shall be recognized. The Apostle Paul in the eleventh chapter of Hebrews names a long list of faithful men who died before the crucifixion of the Lord and before the beginning of the selection of the church. These can never be a part of the heavenly class; they had no heavenly hopes; but God has in store something good for them. ⌜They are to be resurrected as perfect men and constitute the princes or rulers in the earth,⌝ according to his promise. (Psalm 45: 16; Isaiah 32: 1; Matthew 8: 11) ⌜Therefore we may confidently expect that 1925 will mark the return of Abraham,

Isaac, Jacob and the faithful prophets of old, particularly those named by the Apostle in Hebrews chapter eleven, to the condition of human perfection.

RECONSTRUCTION

All the statesmen of the world, all the political economists, all the thoughtful men and women, recognize the fact that the conditions existing prior to the war have passed away and that a new order of things must be put in vogue. All such recognize that this is a period now marking the beginning of reconstruction. The great difficulty is that these men are exercising only human wisdom and have ignored the divine arrangement. We are indeed at the time of reconstruction, the reconstruction not only of a few things, but of all things. The reconstruction will not consist of patching up old and broken down systems and forms and arrangements, but the establishment of a new and righteous one under the great ruler Christ Jesus, the Prince of Peace. The Apostle Peter at Pentecost, speaking under divine inspiration, and referring to that time, said: "Times of refreshing shall come from the presence of the Lord; and he shall send Jesus Christ, which before was preached unto you: whom the heaven must receive [retain] until the times of restitution of all things, which God hath spoken by the mouth of all his holy prophets since the world began". —Acts 3: 19 - 21.

in due time after the establishment of the kingdom. Then it shall come to pass that every one who will keep the saying of the Lord shall never see death. This promise would not have been made by Jesus if he did not intend to carry it into full force and effect in due time.

Again he said: "Whosoever liveth and believeth in me shall never die". (John 11:26) Do we believe the Master's statement? If so, when the time comes for the world to know, then they who believe and, of course, render themselves in obedience to the terms have the absolute and positive statement of Jesus that they shall never die.

Based upon the argument heretofore set forth, then, that the old order of things, the old world, is ending and is therefore passing away, and that the new order is coming in, and that 1925 shall mark the resurrection of the faithful worthies of old and the beginning of reconstruction, it is reasonable to conclude that millions of people now on the earth will be still on the earth in 1925. Then, based upon the promises set forth in the divine Word, we must reach the positive and indisputable conclusion that millions now living will never die.

Of course, it does not mean that every one will live; for some will refuse to obey the divine law; but those who have been evil and turn again to righteousness and obey righteousness shall live and not die. Of this we have the positive statement of the Lord's prophet, as follows:

Millions Now Living Will Never Die, 1920, p. 97

twentieth century an independent study has been carried on that does not blindly follow some traditional chronological calculations of Christendom, and the published timetable resulting from this independent study gives the date of man's creation as 4026 B.C.E.† According to this trustworthy Bible chronology six thousand years from man's creation will end in 1975, and the seventh period of a thousand years of human history will begin in the fall of 1975 C.E.¶

⁴² So six thousand years of man's existence on earth will soon be up, yes, within this generation. Jehovah God is timeless, as it is written in Psalm 90:1, 2: "O Jehovah, you yourself have proved to be a real dwelling for us during generation after generation. Before the mountains themselves were born, or you proceeded to bring forth as with labor pains the earth and the productive land, even from time indefinite to time indefinite you are God." So from the standpoint of Jehovah God these passing six thousand years of man's existence are but as six days of twenty-four hours, for this same psalm (verses 3, 4) goes on to say: "You make mortal man go back to crushed matter, and you say: 'Go back, you sons of men.' For a thousand years are in your eyes but as yesterday when it is past, and as a watch during the night." So in not many years within our own generation we are reaching what Jehovah God could view as the seventh day of man's existence.

Swensko, published in Lund, Sweden, in 1862 (pages CXXI-CXXVIII). This differs from Ussher's Chronology by four years.
† See "Chart of Outstanding Historical Dates" on page 292, in the chapter entitled "Measuring Events in the Stream of Time," of the book *"All Scripture Is Inspired of God and Beneficial,"* published in 1963 by the Watch Tower Bible & Tract Society of Pennsylvania.

42. From the standpoint of Jehovah God, how long has man's existence been?

30   LIFE EVERLASTING—IN FREEDOM OF THE SONS OF GOD

[43] How appropriate it would be for Jehovah God to make of this coming seventh period of a thousand years a sabbath period of rest and release, a great Jubilee sabbath for the proclaiming of liberty throughout the earth to all its inhabitants! This would be most timely for mankind. It would also be most fitting on God's part, for, remember, mankind has yet ahead of it what the last book of the Holy Bible speaks of as the reign of Jesus Christ over earth for a thousand years, the millennial reign of Christ. Prophetically Jesus Christ, when on earth nineteen centuries ago, said concerning himself: "For Lord of the sabbath is what the Son of man is." (Matthew 12:8) It would not be by mere chance or accident but would be according to the loving purpose of Jehovah God for the reign of Jesus Christ, the "Lord of the sabbath," to run parallel with the seventh millennium of man's existence.

[44] The Jubilee year of God's ancient law was a "shadow of the good things to come." The substantial reality that it foreshadowed must yet without fail be introduced for the good of all the groaning human creation. The blessed time for its introduction is fast approaching. Shortly, within our own generation, the symbolical trumpet will be sounded by divine power, proclaiming "liberty in the land to all its inhabitants." (Leviticus 25:8-10) God foresaw the need for this and had it foreshadowed in his ancient law given through the prophet Moses. As his law foreshadowed this coming great worldwide Jubilee, he has laid the full legal basis for its full, glorious realization. Consequently there is now every reason why the human creation will yet be set free, not by men, but by Almighty God. The long-awaited time for this is at hand!

43. What act on God's part would be most timely for mankind and most fitting in the fulfillment of Jehovah's purpose?
44. Why can we have strong confidence that the human creation will yet be set free, not by men, but by God?

Life Everlasting—in Freedom of the Sons of God, 1966, p. 30

494   𝒯ℎ𝑒WATCHTOWER   BROOKLYN, N.Y.

ed to be October 5 (Julian) or September 29 (Gregorian) 537 B.C.E.—Ezra 1:1-4; 3:1-6.

[24] Here, then, very definitely established, is another milestone—the time when the seventy years of desolation of the land of Judah came to an end—about October 1, 537. (Jer. 25:11, 12; 29:10) It is now a simple formula to determine when the seventy years began. One has only to add

70 to 537 to get 607. So about October 1, 607 B.C.E., the desolating of the land of Judah and the complete emptying out of its inhabitants was fully accomplished.

[25] The importance of the year 607 B.C.E. in this Biblical chronology will become more apparent in the following article, as we seek an answer to the provocative question, When was Adam created?

---

24. So when did the seventy years of desolation begin, and when did they end?

25. The answer to what question is related to the year 607 B.C.E.?

WHY ARE YOU LOOKING FORWARD TO 1975?

WHAT about all this talk concerning the year 1975? Lively discussions, some based on speculation, have burst into flame during recent months among serious students of the Bible. Their interest has been kindled by the belief that 1975 will mark the end of 6,000 years of human history since Adam's creation. The nearness of such an important date indeed fires the imagination and presents unlimited possibilities for discussion.

[2] But wait! How do we know their calculations are correct? What basis is there for saying Adam was created nearly 5,993 years ago? Does the one Book that can be implicitly trusted for its truthful historical accuracy, namely, the Inspired Word of Jehovah, the Holy Bible, give support and credence to such a conclusion?

[3] In the marginal references of the Protestant *Authorized* or *King James Version,* and in the footnotes of certain editions of the Catholic *Douay* version, the date of man's creation is said to be 4004 B.C.E. This marginal date, however, is no part of the inspired text of the Holy Scriptures, since it was first suggested more than fifteen centuries after the last Bible writer died, and was not added to any edition of the Bible until 1701 C.E. It is an insertion based upon the conclusions of an Irish prelate, the Anglican Archbishop James Ussher (1581-1656). Ussher's chronology was only one of the many sincere efforts made during the past centuries to determine the time of Adam's creation. A hundred years ago when a count was taken, no less than 140 different timetables had been published by se-

---

1, 2. (a) What has sparked special interest in the year 1975, and with what results? (b) But what questions are raised?

3. Is the date for Adam's creation as found in many copies of the Bible part of the inspired Scriptures, and do all agree on the date?

in which Adam was created. Since man naturally began to count time with his own beginning, and since man's most ancient calendars started each year in the autumn, it is reasonable to assume that the first man Adam was created in the fall of the year.

[28] Thus, through a careful independent study by dedicated Bible scholars who have pursued the subject for a number of years, and who have not blindly followed some traditional chronological calculations of Christendom, we have arrived at a date for Adam's creation that is 22 years more distant in the past than Ussher's figure. This means time is running out two decades sooner than traditional chronology anticipates.

[29] After much of the mathematics and genealogies, really, of what benefit is this information to us today? Is it not all dead history, as uninteresting and profitless as walking through a cemetery copying old dates off tombstones? After all, why should we be any more interested in the date of Adam's creation than in the birth of King Tut? Well, for one thing, if 4,026 is added to 1,968 (allowing for the lack of a zero year between C.E. and B.C.E.) one gets a total of 5,993 years, come this autumn, since Adam's creation. That means, in the fall of the year 1975, a little over seven years from now (and not in 1997 as would be the case if Ussher's figures were correct), it will be 6,000 years since the creation of Adam, the father of all mankind!

ADAM CREATED AT CLOSE OF "SIXTH DAY"

[30] Are we to assume from this study that the battle of Armageddon will be all over by the autumn of 1975, and the long-looked-for thousand-year reign of Christ will begin by then? Possibly, but we wait to see how closely the seventh thousand-year period of man's existence coincides with the sabbathlike thousand-year reign of Christ. If these two periods run parallel with each other as to the calendar year, it will not be by mere chance or accident but will be according to Jehovah's loving and timely purposes. Our chronology, however, which is reasonably accurate (but admittedly not infallible), at the best only points to the autumn of 1975 as the end of 6,000 years of man's existence on earth. It does not necessarily mean that 1975 marks the end of the first 6,000 years of Jehovah's seventh creative "day." Why not? Because after his creation Adam lived some time during the "sixth day," which unknown amount of time would need to be subtracted from Adam's 930 years, to determine when the sixth seven-thousand-year period or "day" ended, and how long Adam lived into the "seventh day." And yet the end of that sixth creative "day" could end within the same Gregorian calendar year of Adam's creation. It may involve only a difference of weeks or months, not years.

[31] In regard to Adam's creation it is good to read carefully what the Bible says. Moses in compiling the book of Genesis referred to written records or "histories" that predated the Flood. The first of these begins with Genesis 1:1 and ends at Genesis 2:4 with the words, "This is the history of the heavens and the earth . . . " The second historical document begins with Genesis 2:5 and ends with verse two of chapter five. Hence we have two separate accounts of creation from slightly different points of view. In the second of these accounts, in Genesis 2:19, the original Hebrew verb translated "was forming" is in the progressive imperfect form. This does not mean that the animals and birds

---

28. How does this chronology differ from Ussher's in regard to Adam's creation?
29. Why be concerned with the date of Adam's creation?
30. What may occur before 1975, but what attitude should we take?

---

31. What do the first two chapters of Genesis disclose?

HOW ARE YOU USING YOUR LIFE?

IS IT not apparent that most of mankind are living their lives for themselves? They are using their lives as *they* see fit, without concern for others. But what about us? The apostle Paul wrote to fellow servants of Jehovah, saying: "None of us, in fact, lives with regard to himself only, and no one dies with regard to himself only; for both if we live, we live to Jehovah, and if we die, we die to Jehovah. Therefore both if we live and if we die, we belong to Jehovah."—Rom. 14:7, 8.

This is something for all of us to give serious thought to: It would be entirely inappropriate for us, while professing to be Jehovah's people, to try to live our lives with regard to ourselves only. As the apostle Paul wrote: "You do not belong to yourselves, for you were bought with a price. By all means, glorify God."—1 Cor. 6:19, 20.

Are we not thankful that Jehovah God has purchased us and that we now belong to Him? He has bought us with the life of his own dear Son so that eternal death does not have to be our lot, but we have before us the opportunity to enjoy everlasting life. (John 3:16, 36) How are you affected by this loving provision of God? Does it not cause you to want to show Jehovah your deep appreciation? The apostle Peter noted that if we have the proper mental disposition we will be moved to "live the remainder of [our] time in the flesh, no more for the desires of men, *but for God's will.*"—1 Pet. 4:2.

Is that what you are doing? Are you living no longer simply to satisfy personal ambitions or desires, but to do God's will? Are there ways in which you could share more fully in doing the will of God?

God's Will for Us

Jehovah makes clear in his Word that his will for us today includes accomplishing a great work of Kingdom-preaching before the end of this system comes. (Matt. 24:14) Jesus Christ did a similar work. He said: "Also to other cities I must declare the good news of the kingdom of God, *because for this I was sent forth.*"—Luke 4:43.

Jesus did not hold back, but was wholesouled in his service to God. When we read the historical accounts of his ministry in the Gospels, how impressed we are with his energy and zeal in doing the Kingdom-preaching! Jesus knew that he had only a short time, and he did not spare himself in finishing his assignment. Should we not today be imitating his example, especially since we have such a short time left now in which to complete the Kingdom-preaching?

Yes, the end of this system is so very near! Is that not reason to increase our activity? In this regard we can learn something from a runner who puts on a final burst of speed near the finish of a race. Look at Jesus, who apparently stepped up his activity during his final days on earth. In fact, over 27 percent of the material in the Gospels is devoted to just the last week of Jesus' earthly ministry!—Matt. 21:1–27:50; Mark 11:1–15: 37; Luke 19:29–23:46; John 11:55–19:30.

By carefully and prayerfully examining our own circumstances, we also may find that we can spend more time and energy in preaching during this final period before the present system ends. Many of our brothers and sisters are doing just that. This is evident from the rapidly increasing number of pioneers.

Yes, since the summer of 1973 there have been new peaks in pioneers every month. Now there are 20,394 regular and special pioneers in the United States, an all-time peak. That is 5,190 more than there were in February 1973! A 34-percent increase! Does that not warm our hearts? Reports are heard of brothers selling their homes and property and planning to finish out the rest of their days in this old system in the pioneer service. Certainly this is a fine way to spend the short time remaining before the wicked world's end.—1 John 2:17.

Circumstances such as poor health or responsibilities in connection with your family may limit what you can do in the field ministry. And yet, the pioneer ranks include many who have health limitations, as well as some persons with families. But these broth-

KINGDOM MINISTRY, MAY 1974   3

8

A Changing "Channel"

While a prophet is often thought of as one who tells the future, a more general meaning can include the thought of being a divine spokesman or mouthpiece. The Watchtower Society claims this role for itself, too, and in fact asserts that it is the sole and exclusive channel of communication that God is using:

> . . . Jehovah God has also provided his visible organization, his "faithful and discreet slave," made up of spirit-anointed ones . . . Unless we are in touch with this channel of communication that God is using, we will not progress along the road to life, no matter how much Bible reading we do. . . (*The Watchtower*, 12/1/81, page 27 [*see* p. 81]).

Many religious groups change their doctrines and practices, to some extent, over the years. This is inevitable, in part, because the surrounding social, political and cultural influences do not remain the same, and in part because new leaders within the sect see things differently. But the Watchtower Society claims that its changes in belief and practice result, not from such mundane forces, but from God Himself providing "new light" or "new truths" through His "channel of communication." Thus Witnesses are always reminded to "move ahead with Jehovah's organization" (*The Watchtower*, 6/1/67, p. 335).

If the Watchtower Society were really God's channel, the sort of changes it would undergo would be different from those of "worldly" organizations. For example, there would not be the sort of back-and-forth policy shifts that we see in civil government when a Democratic administration is voted out in favor of a Republican administration, only to be followed again in a few years by another Democratic administration. Instead there would always be forward progress in the general direction of closer conformity to God's will. And God would not reveal through his channel any "new truths" that contradict "truths" he revealed yesterday.

The Watchtower acknowledges these proper expectations. Long ago it said:

> If we were following a *man* undoubtedly it would be different with us; undoubtedly one human idea would contradict another and that which was light one or two or six years ago would be regarded as darkness now; But with God there is no variableness, neither shadow of turning, and so it is with *truth*; any knowledge or light coming from God must be like its author. A new view of truth never can contradict a former truth. *"New light"* never extinguishes older *"light,"* but adds to it. . . (*Zion's Watch Tower*, February, 1881, p. 3 [see p. 82–83]).

And yet, the organization has in fact done just what it said should not be done: it has introduced many "new truths" that contradicted what it had earlier been proclaiming as "truth." An outstanding example of this is found in the teachings on the Great Pyramid of Egypt.

For nearly fifty years, from 1879 through 1928, the Watchtower Society taught that the Pyramid was "God's stone Witness and Prophet" [see p. 84], inspired much like the Bible, and an object to be studied by Christians to gain knowledge of future events. Thus, the book *Thy Kingdom Come* (*Studies in the Scriptures*, vol. III), published by the Society in 1891, features numerous diagrams of pyramid chambers and passageways, along with their measurements. Pyramid inches are translated into calendar years in a complex timetable of the "Divine plan." Chapter 10 of this book is titled "The Testimony of God's Stone Witness and Prophet, the Great Pyramid in Egypt" (page 313, edition of 1903, [see p. 84]). It says:

. . . the Great Pyramid . . . seems in a remarkable manner to teach, in harmony with all the prophets, an outline of the plan of God, past, present, and future. . . (p. 314, [*see* p. 85]).

Some might wish to pass off this devotion to the pyramid as a quirk of the Society's founder and first president, Charles Taze Russell. However, years after Russell's death in 1916 and well into the 1920s the organization continued to teach that God designed the Great Pyramid:

In the passages of the Great Pyramid of Gizeh the agreement of one or two measurements with the present-truth chronology might seem accidental, but the correspondency of dozens of measurements proves that the same God designed both pyramid and plan. . . (*The Watchtower*, 6/5/22, p. 187 [*see* p.86–87]).

The great Pyramid of Egypt, standing as a silent and inanimate witness of the Lord, is a messenger; and its testimony speaks with great eloquence concerning the divine plan. . . (*The Watchtower*, 5/15/25, p. 148 [*see* p. 88–89]).

But then, in 1928, the Society completely reversed its teaching on the pyramid, now calling it "Satan's Bible" and declaring that persons following pyramid teachings were "not following after Christ":

If the pyramid is not mentioned in the Bible, then following its teachings is being led by vain philosophy and false science and not following after Christ (*The Watchtower*, 11/15/28, p. 341 [*see* p. 90]).

It is more reasonable to conclude that the great pyramid of Gizeh, as well as the other pyramids thereabout, also the sphinx, were built by the rulers of Egypt and under the direction of Satan the Devil. . . . Then Satan put his knowledge in dead stone, which may be called Satan's Bible, and not God's stone witness. . . (*The Watchtower*, 11/15/28, p. 344 [*see* p. 91]).

First it was designed by God; then, by the devil. First it was God's witness and prophet; then, Satan's Bible. What more dramatic example could there be of a "new truth" that contradicted prior teachings? In fact, if what *The Watchtower* said in 1928 was correct, then much of what it had been teaching for the preceding fifty years had been taken from "Satan's Bible" and communicated by people who were "not following after Christ." Was it truly God's channel of communication during that time, or the devil's?

In order to excuse a number of such doctrinal reversals over the years, Jehovah's Witnesses will often turn in their Bibles to Proverbs 4:18 and read, "But the path of the righteous ones is like the bright light that is getting lighter and lighter until the day is firmly established" (NWT). Since the changes indicate that their "light" is getting "brighter," they see this as evidence that they are the "righteous ones," that is, God's chosen channel.

However what if, after the "light" has gotten "brighter," the organization then returns to the darkness it had been in before? What if it returns to a teaching that had previously been rejected in favor of "new light"? The Watchtower Society has done this very thing on a number of occasions. One that older Witnesses alive today should remember involves the significance of Romans 13:1—"Let every soul be in subjection to the superior authorities. . ." (NWT). To whom should everyone be in subjection? Around the time of World War I the teaching was that the superior authorities were the earthly political governments. Later this was rejected in favor of a "new truth", namely, that the superior authorities were "Jehovah God and Christ Jesus." (*"Make Sure of All Things"*, 1953 edition, p. 369 [*see* p. 92]). During the 1950s, Jehovah's Witnesses looked back at the prior teaching and said:

> When the Society began to be freed for further preaching work following World War I, they soon realized that they had been held in spiritual bondage too in many ways. There were many false doctrines and practices that had not yet been cleaned out of the organization. . . . With considerable misunderstanding they had accepted earthly political governments as the "superior authorities" that God had ordained according to Romans 13:1 . . . particularly the civil rulers. . . . (*Jehovah's Witnesses in the Divine Purpose*, 1959, p. 91 [*see* p. 93]).

This "false doctrine" had been "cleaned out of the organization" by the 1950s, but in the 1960s it was reintroduced: "Who are the 'superior authorities' to whom Christians are to be in subjection? The duly constituted political governments of this world" (*The Watchtower*, 1/1/63, p. 31 [*see* p. 94]).

To help your JW loved one see the seriousness of such back-and-forth doctrinal changes, you might intersperse the discussion with questions such as:

> If you had been a Witness at that time, what response would have been expected from you when the Society reversed its teaching?
>
> Would you have been put on trial and disfellowshiped if you failed to change your mind when the leaders changed theirs?
>
> Were some people back then expelled for believing what the Society later took up teaching again?
>
> When the Society again taught the formerly rejected view as "truth," did it welcome back the men and women who held to that "truth" all along, but who had been disfellowshiped for believing it during the time the Society was teaching differently?

If you or I were to vacillate doctrinally in this way on our own, changing our mind back and forth as to what we believed, it could be blamed on "human nature" or chalked up to experience as part of our spiritual growth. But if a group claiming to be God's mouthpiece engages in doctrinal flip-flops, those actions seriously undermine the validity of its pretensions. Has the Watchtower Society negated its claim to be God's "channel of communication" by some of the messages it has communicated? With others in mind, *The Watchtower* of May 15, 1976, made this observation:

> It is a serious matter to represent God and Christ in one way, then find that our understanding of the major teachings and fundamental doctrines of the Scriptures was in error, and then after that, to go back to the very doctrines that, by years of study, we had thoroughly determined to be in error. Christians cannot be vacillating—wishy-washy—about such fundamental teachings. What confidence can one put in the sincerity or judgment of such persons? (p. 298 [*see* p. 95]).

Not only has the Watchtower Society shown itself capable of going back to doctrines that it had "thoroughly determined to be in error," but there are even cases of the organization flip-flopping back and forth on the same issue a number of times. A prime example of this is the question of whether or not the men of Sodom and Gomorrah will be resurrected. The official teaching on this from 'God's channel':

Yes	No
1879 (see p. 96–97)	1952 (see p. 98)
1965 (see p. 99)	1988 (see p. 100–101)

(These page numbers refer to *Watchtower* issues of July, 1879, p. 8; June 1, 1952, p. 338; August 1, 1965, p. 479; and June 1, 1988, p. 31.)

At a time when a few dissenters left the group, calling attention to many such doctrinal flip-flops over the years, the Watchtower sought to defend itself, as follows:

> . . . At times explanations given by Jehovah's visible organization have shown adjustments, seemingly to previous points of view. But this has not actually been the case. This might be compared to what is known in navigational circles as "tacking." By maneuvering the sails the sailors can cause a ship to go from right to left, back and forth, but all the time making progress toward their destination in spite of contrary winds. . . (*The Watchtower*, 12/1/81, p. 27 [see p. 81]).

Next to this denial of any adjustments back to "previous points of view" the magazine featured an illustration of a sailboat traveling in a zig-zag course. But, as we have seen above, the Society has actually returned to previous points of view, and then abandoned them again. Instead of their "light" getting "brighter," it has actually been blinking on and off. Rather than "tacking into the wind," a more accurate description would be that given in their *New World Translation* of the Bible at Ephesians 4:14, . . . "tossed about as by waves and carried hither and thither by every wind of teaching by means of the trickery of men, by means of cunning in contriving error." *The Living Bible* paraphrases it this way: . . . "forever changing our minds about what we believe because someone has told us something different, or has cleverly lied to us and made the lie sound like the truth."

the pathway that Jehovah's servants must tread.—2 Sam. 23:3, 4.

² However, it may have seemed to some as though that path has not always gone straight forward. ⌐At times explanations given by Jehovah's visible organization have shown adjustments, seemingly to previous points of view. But this has not actually been the case. This might be compared to what is known in navigational circles as "tacking." By maneuvering the sails the sailors can cause a ship to go from right to left, back and forth, but all the time making progress toward their destination in spite of contrary winds.¬ And that goal in view for Jehovah's servants is the "new heavens and a new earth" of God's promise.—2 Pet. 3:13.

³ There is no question that Jehovah God is continuing to bless the global activity of his witnesses, as directed by the "faithful and discreet slave." This can be seen by the fruits. Remember, Jesus said: "Every good tree produces fine fruit." And such righteous fruits are to be seen internationally today in one people only—the united, global society of Jehovah's Witnesses.—Matt. 7:17.

⁴ No matter where we may live on earth, God's Word continues to serve as a light to our path and a lamp to our roadway as to our conduct and beliefs. (Ps. 119:105) But ⌐Jehovah God has also provided his visible organization, his "faithful and discreet slave," made up of spirit-anointed ones,¬ to help Christians in all nations to understand and apply properly the Bible in their lives.⌐Unless we are in touch with this channel of communication that God is using, we will not progress along the road to life, no matter how much Bible reading we do¬—Compare Acts 8:30-40.

Tacking into the Wind

⁵ Regarding God's channel of communication, Jesus said that the "faithful and discreet slave" would provide spiritual nourishment at the right time for all his followers and that he would set this "slave" over all his belongings. (Matt. 24:45-47) It is also noteworthy that the apostle Paul, at Ephesians 4:11-16, indicated that the Christian congregation needed not only such inspired instruments as apostles and prophets but also evangelizers, shepherds and teachers to help Christians to arrive at the oneness in the faith and the accurate knowledge of the Son of God, and to gain full spiritual maturity.—See also 1 Corinthians 1:10; Philippians 1:9-11.

⁶ This "faithful and discreet slave,"

2. How may we regard periodic adjustments in viewpoint?
3. What evidence is there that Jehovah is continuing to bless his witnesses?
4, 5. In addition to his inspired Word, what other instrument has Jehovah God used to guide his people?

6. Because of what factors has it been necessary at times to reevaluate viewpoints?

The Watchtower, 12/1/81, page 27

structed concerning the evil day, there is the intimation that it will be a time of special trial, and admonitions to held fast, &c., are given as in this 38th verse. During the last six or seven years, the Lord has been leading us, his people, in a very remarkable manner. As we look backward we can see that our pathway has been as "a shining light . . . . shining more and more." It has been *progressive*, bringing us strength with "meat in due season." It has caused us to grow both in *grace and knowledge* and this growth, taken in connection with the fact that we are not obliged to look back—and now call *darkness* what was then called by some of the brethren, "a great flood of light," is the very strongest grounds for confidence that the same Lord who then supplied us *light* from the word, is still providing of the same kind. We say then, "Cast not away your confidence" in *our Leader*, "the great Shepherd of the sheep."

If we were following *a man* undoubtedly it would be different with us; undoubtedly one human idea would contradict another and that which was light one or two or six years ago would be regarded as darkness now: But with God there is no variableness, neither shadow of turning, and so it is with *truth*; any knowledge or light coming from God must be like its author. A new view of truth never can contradict a former truth. "*New light*" never extinguishes older "*light*," but adds to it. If you were lighting up a building containing seven gas jets you would not extinguish one every time you lighted another, but would add one light to another and they would be in harmony and thus give increase of light: So is it with the light of truth; the true increase is by adding to, not by substituting one for another.

Therefore, in mentioning grounds of our confidence that we are in the shining path under the leading of the Spirit, we mention first that the tendency of present truth is to produce the proper fruit of the spirit, of which love is the chief. The tendency of our growth in knowledge is to growth in grace. "He that hath this hope in him *purifieth himself* even as he (Jesus) is pure." Our pathway has been one of increase of light in harmony with former light. Thus let us have been led to increased confidence in our leader. Let us take

A GLANCE BACKWARD

at the steps of progress, and let all notice that the progress is not only forward but *upward; i. e.,* the tendency is from the

Ark, and *understood not* till the Deluge came and swept them all away; thus will be the *presence of the Son of Man.*"

His surprise was, at finding that the Greek word *parousia* which signifies *presence*, had in our common version been improperly rendered *coming*, but the new rendering showed that it was not the act of coming that resembled the days of Noah, but that as in Noah's days the masses of the people "*knew not*," so it would be in the time of Jesus' *presence* at the second advent. Humanity will go on eating, drinking, marrying, etc., as usual and "know not" that he is *present*. The next step was, to see whether the account of the same discourse as recorded by Luke, would harmonize with this new idea of *a presence* unseen, except by the eye of faith, until the "little flock" typified by Noah had gone from among men into the condition of safety (from the coming storm) represented by the Ark—"one taken and another left."

Luke's account was in perfect accord with Matthew's, though in different words—"As it was *in the days of Noah* so shall it be also *in the days of the Son of Man.*" (Luke xvii:26.)

This was communicated to others of the disappointed ones, and with the remembrance that the time arguments above referred to had been found faultless and unalterable and proved that Jesus was due here in the fall of 1874, came the thought—Can it be possible that Jesus does not come in a fleshly body at his second advent? Can it be possible that his *presence* began at the time indicated in those prophecies, and yet we went on eating and drinking, etc., and "*knew not*" of his presence?

A careful examination of the Word was begun by all deeply interested, to see whether it, as a whole, would be in harmony with this new thought. It was found to be in perfect harmony and opened up and made clear many scriptures hitherto dark: For instance the differences between *natural, earthly* bodies and *spiritual, heavenly* bodies; how that the things which are seen are temporal, natural, but the things that are not seen are eternal, spiritual; that spiritual beings could not be seen by mortals, (without a miracle) and that the object and scope of the Gospel age was, the taking out of the world of mankind a "little flock" to be associated with Jesus in the work of the future—destroying evil and blessing all the families of the earth; that God's plan was not, to natural to the spiritual. We will look, not at any one person's experience, but at what serves to show the advance of the knowledge of truth for ten years past. Looking back to 1871, we see that many of our company were what are known as Second Adventists, and the light they held briefly stated, was that there would be a second advent of Jesus—that he would come to bless and immortalize the saints, to judge the world and to burn up the world and all the wicked. This, they claimed would occur in 1873, because the 6,000 years from the creation of Adam were complete then.

Well, 1873 came, the end of 6,000 years, and yet no *burning* of the world, &c. But prophecies were found which pointed positively to 1874 as the time when Jesus was due to be present, and the resurrection of Daniel was also due as proved by the ending of jubilee cycles and the 1335 days of Dan. xii. The autumn of 1874, anxiously expected, finally came, but the earth rolled on as ever. "All things continued as they were from the beginning of creation." All their hearts were sad. They said, "Surely we have been in error—but where? Surely it is clearly taught that Jesus will come again; perhaps our calculation of time is at fault." Carefully they examined the chronology but it seemed faultless and positively declared that the 6,000 years ended in 1873. Then the prophetic arguments were carefully re-examined. Was an error found? No, they stood the test of all investigation and the jubilee argument and "1335 days," of Daniel could not possibly be prolonged beyond the fall of '74 or the spring of 1875 and these periods were both past.

Dark indeed seemed the outlook; all were discouraged. It had seemed as though the Lord had been leading in the past, and yet now all these things which had been thought light seemed to be proved darkness.

Just at this time Bro. Keith, (one of our contributors) was used of the Lord to throw another beam of *light* on the subject which brought order out of confusion, and caused all of the former "light" to shine with tenfold brightness. Brother K. had been reading, carefully Matt. xxiv chapter, using the "Emphatic Diaglott," a new and very exact word for word translation of the New Testament; when he came to the 37th and 39th verses he was much surprised to find that it read as follows, viz.: "For as the days of Noah thus will be the *presence* of the son of man. For as in those days, those before the deluge they were eating and drinking, marrying and pledging in marriage till the day that Noah entered the

destroy all mankind after the gathering of the Gospel church but to "*restore all things*" and destroy only the evil which now rules in the world; that the *fire* supposed to be literal, was really symbolic and signified a great time of trouble which would be the close of the Gospel age and dawn of the Millennial in which all evil principles of governments and society would be manifested and destroyed, as a necessary preparation for the coming blessing.

So says the Prophet: "Wait ye upon me, saith the Lord, until *the day* that I rise up to the prey, for my determination is to gather the nations, that I may assemble the kingdoms and pour upon them mine indignation even *all* my fierce anger for all the earth, *shall be devoured with the fire of my jealousy:* For then will I turn to the people a pure language and they shall all call upon the name of the Lord to serve him with one consent." (Zeph. iii:8-9.)

As to the manner of Christ's coming other scriptures were found to be in perfect accord with the accounts of Matt. and Luke, of its being an *unseen presence:* For instance, the angel's message—Acts i. 11.

"THIS SAME JESUS SHALL SO COME IN LIKE MANNER as ye have seen him go into heaven." This had generally been supposed to teach that Jesus would come *in the flesh,* and be *seen* of men, as he was there seen of the disciples. But when carefully examined the text does not say that any one will *see* him, but that he will so come as he went away not with "flaming fire" and rolling thunder and great outward demonstration, but silently, *unknown* to the world. And if he "so comes in like manner," how much in harmony with Matthew's and Luke's record—they will eat and drink and know not of his *presence.*

But the angels' language seemed peculiar—this *same* Jesus as though there had been *another* Jesus: Examination revealed the fact, that Jesus since his resurrection is a totally different being from the Jesus who died; that a great change had taken place. While before his death he had been the "*man* Christ Jesus," having the form of a servant and perfect human powers, etc., and yet none but human powers, except as the Father's power was operated and manifested through him: (John xiv. 10.) Yet now, since his resurrection he claims *divine powers* not as the Father in him, but as his own, saying—"All power in heaven and in earth is given unto *me*" and he is no longer a natural, but a spiritual body. It was sown a natural body, raised a spiritual body—sown mor-

[188]

CHAPTER X.

THE TESTIMONY OF GOD'S STONE WITNESS AND PROPHET, THE GREAT PYRAMID IN EGYPT.

GENERAL DESCRIPTION OF THE GREAT PYRAMID.—WHY OF SPECIAL INTEREST TO CHRISTIANS.—THE GREAT PYRAMID A STOREHOUSE OF TRUTH—SCIENTIFIC, HISTORIC AND PROPHETIC.—BIBLE ALLUSIONS TO IT.—WHY, WHEN AND BY WHOM BUILT.—IMPORTANCE OF ITS LOCATION.—ITS SCIENTIFIC LESSONS.—ITS TESTIMONY CONCERNING THE PLAN OF REDEMPTION—THE PLAN OF THE AGES. —THE DEATH AND THE RESURRECTION OF CHRIST INDICATED.—THE DOWN-WARD COURSE OF THE WORLD, ENDING IN A GREAT TIME OF TROUBLE.—THE NATURE OF THE TROUBLE. — THE GREAT REFORMATION MOVEMENT MARKED. —LENGTH OF THE JEWISH AGE INDICATED.—THE "HIGH CALLING" OF THE GOSPEL CHURCH SHOWN.—THE COURSE OF THE CHURCH'S CONSECRATION.— THE END OF THE HIGH CALLING MARKED. DATE OF THE SECOND ADVENT OF CHRIST.—HOW RESTITUTION BLESSINGS FOR THE WORLD ARE INDICATED.— THE COURSE OF THE WORLD DURING THE MILLENNIAL AGE.—ITS END.—CON-TRAST OF THE TWO CONDITIONS, HUMAN AND SPIRITUAL, AS INDICATED IN THE PYRAMID.—THE PYRAMID REFUTES ATHEISM, INFIDELITY AND ALL EVOLUTION THEORIES, AND VERIFIES BOTH THE PLAN OF THE BIBLE AND ITS APPOINTED TIMES AND SEASONS.

"In that day shall there be an altar to the Lord in the midst of the land of Egypt, and a pillar at the border thereof to the Lord. And it shall be for a sign and for a witness unto the Lord of hosts in the land of Egypt."—Isa. 19: 19, 20.

THE ancients recounted seven wonders of the world, and at the very head of the list named the Great Pyramid of Gizeh. It is situated in Egypt, not far from the present city of Cairo. No other building in the world equals it in size. One of the leading granite men of this country, who made a personal inspection of the Great Pyramid, says: "There are blocks of stone in the Pyramid which weigh three or four times as much as one of the obelisks. I saw

313

Thy Kingdom Come (*Studies in the Scriptures,* vol. III), 1891, edition of 1903, page 313

314   *Thy Kingdom Come.*

a stone whose estimated weight was 880 tons.   There are stones in it thirty feet in length which fit so closely together that you may run a penknife over the surface without discovering the breaks between them.   They are not laid with mortar, either.   There is now no machinery so perfect that it will make two surfaces thirty feet in length which will meet together as these wonderful stones in the Great Pyramid meet.''   It covers an area of about thirteen acres.   It is 486 feet high and 764 feet broad at its base.   It is estimated that the Great Pyramid weighs six million tons, and that to remove it would require sixty thousand steam engines, each drawing one hundred tons.   In fact, the wealth of Egypt is not sufficient to pay laborers to demolish it.   From these facts it is evident that, whoever was its great designer, he intended that it should be an enduring monument.

Viewed from whatever standpoint we please, ⌐the Great Pyramid⌐ is certainly the most remarkable building in the world ; but in the light of an investigation which has been in progress for the past thirty–two years, it acquires new interest to every Christian advanced in the study of God's Word ; for it ⌐seems in a remarkable manner to teach, in harmony with all the prophets, an outline of the plan of God, past, present and future.⌐

It should be remembered that, aside from the Great Pyramid here referred to, there are others, some of stone and some of brick ; but all of them are mere attempts to copy it, and are in every way inferior—in size, accuracy and internal arrangement.   And it has also been demonstrated that, unlike the Great Pyramid, they contain no symbolic features, but were evidently designed and used as sepulchers for the royal families of Egypt.

The Great Pyramid, however, proves to be a storehouse of important truth—scientific, historic and prophetic—and its testimony is found to be in perfect accord with the Bible, their time on "science [knowledge] falsely so called" (1 Timothy 6:20), when God has provided *a chronological bridge*, over the indecipherable pagan chronology of the prehistoric period in question, in the shape of prophecy and fulfillment of "seventy years' desolation"? It is another divinely-furnished bridge like that over the period of the Judges. (Acts 13:19-21) It would be a foolish waste of time to attempt to work out the detailed chronology of the Judges; and it is equally wasteful to cast aside the divinely-given bridge over the seventy-year period of desolation and to try to establish connected, detailed facts from pagan sources; for that, in fact, is what is implied by reliance upon the currently accepted notions about the chronology of Babylonia copied in all encyclopedias and reference works from the same unreliable source.

FURTHER PROOF OF PRESENT-TRUTH CHRONOLOGY

There is a well known law of mathematics called "the law of probabilities". Applications of this law are frequent in everyday life in settling matters of doubt. In a family of children, if a certain kind of mischief is committed, the probabilities— indeed, the certainty— are that it was done by a certain one, and that the others assuredly did not do it. If some peculiar damage is done by night to a single house, then by the law of probabilities it may have been a pure accident; if done to two houses in the same manner it probably was not accidental but by design of some person; but if done to

consecrated child of God may, endeavor to search out things to come.—I Peter 1:11, 12; John 16:13.

It is not necessary to show how if a change of 19 years were made in the chronology the time from Jacob to Jesus would become shortened from 1845 to 1826 years, and the entire system of dates based on the "Jewish parallels" would collapse; how the jubilee system dates would fall out of place from its present symmetry; how the 2520-year parallels would disappear; how the entire system of dates would be scattered; how there could be no foundation for faith in the resulting chronological jumble; and how there could be no sound reason for believing in the presence of the Lord, the place and work of Pastor Russell, the end of the age, the harvest work, or in any of the literature published by the Society. Many years ago all these matters were deeply considered by Pastor Russell, and he declared, in an article which we will soon republish, that a change of one year would destroy the entire system of chronology.

PRESENT-TRUTH CHRONOLOGY IS CORRECT

We have shown that the present-truth chronology is correct and others are incorrect because:

(1) It is based squarely on inspired prophecy.
(2) The fulfillment is recorded in the Bible and in the history of God's chosen people, the Jews.
(3) The seventy years are all years of desolation.
(4) There was no captivity and no vassalage of Judah

three or more houses in the same manner it passes out of the possibility of accident into the *certainty* of design.

The chronology of present truth might be a mere happening if it were not for the repetitions in the two great cycles of 1845 and 2520 years, which take it out of the realm of chance and into that of certainty. If there were only one or two corresponding dates in these cycles, they might possibly be mere coincidences, but where the agreements of dates and events come by the dozens, they cannot possibly be by chance, but must be by the design or plan of the only personal Being capable of such a plan—Jehovah himself; *and the chronology itself must be right.*

In the passages of the Great Pyramid of Gizeh the agreement of one or two measurements with the present-truth chronology might be accidental, but the correspondency of dozens of measurements proves that the same God designed both pyramid and plan—and at the same time proves the correctness of the chronology.

The agreement of the chronology with certain measurements of the Tabernacle and the Temple of Ezekiel further stamps the chronology as true.

It is on the basis of such and so many correspondencies—in accordance with the soundest laws known to science—that we affirm that, *Scripturally, scientifically, and historically, present-truth chronology is correct beyond a doubt.* Its reliability has been abundantly confirmed by the dates and events of 1874, 1914, and 1918. Present-truth chronology is a secure basis on which the

in 625 B. C. from which to count the seventy years captivity or servitude.

(5) Pagan "history" on the subject is unreliable.

(6) The opinions of "authorities" on this pagan "history" are guesses and conjectures.

(7) The monumental inscriptions are untrustworthy because of the untruthfulness and unreliability of the demon-worshiping and demon-controlled pagan monarchs.

(8) The inscriptions omit some important facts and falsify others.

(9) The archeologists are not conscientious or honest in presenting the inscriptions.

(10) Reliance upon pagan history or archæology leads through worse doubts and ever more of them, into infidelity.

(11) Present-truth chronology is correct beyond the possibility of a doubt.

Present-truth chronology is based upon divine prophecy and its Biblical fulfillment, that the seventy years were years of desolation, not part desolation and part captivity. The chronology stands firm as a rock, based upon the Word of God.

It is a matter of faith in Jehovah and in his inspired Word. (2 Timothy 3:16) Those that lack faith in God's Word and cast about for needless help from admittedly lying pagan records, will doubtless receive according to their lack of faith. Those that stick closely to the Word will receive according to their faith.

upon the holy mountain of God; thou hast walked up and down in the midst of the stones of fire. Thou wast perfect in thy ways from the day that thou wast created, till iniquity was found in thee."—Ezekiel 28:14, 15.

[11] Lucifer was commissioned to do certain work in God's organization; but instead of being obedient he became lawless. Doubtless he was one of the morning stars mentioned in the prophecy of Job. (Job 38:7) In the organization of Jehovah there are cherubim and seraphim.—Genesis 3:24; Isaiah 6:2.

[12] Adam, when a perfect creature in Eden, was a part of God's organization; and to him was committed certain work to do. (Genesis 1:28) When Israel was organized into a nation and God made a covenant with them through Moses as mediator, that nation became a part of God's organization, authorized to do certain things. (Exodus 19:6, 7) Israel's course of training foreshadowed the training of the new creation.

[13] The highest position in God's organization he evidently left vacant until he had put certain tests upon his creatures. The Logos met all these tests, and of him it is written: "Thou lovest righteousness, and hatest wickedness: therefore God, thy God, hath anointed thee with the oil of gladness above thy fellows."—Psalm 45:7; Hebrews 1:9.

ALL MESSENGERS

[14] The Church, which is the Body of Christ, is of

GREATEST ANGEL

[18] It was Jesus who said: "He that is greatest among you, shall be your servant." (Matthew 23:11) The greatest and most honorable messenger of Jehovah, the special angel of God, was the Logos, Jesus, the only begotten Son of God. Early in his ministry he said: "My meat is to do the will of him that sent me, and to finish his work." "I know him: for I am from him, and he hath sent me." (John 4:34; 7:29) He was sent on a special mission from the Father to open the way to life and immortality.—John 10:10; 2 Tim. 1:11.

[19] It seems quite clear from the Scriptures that long prior to his human existence Jesus, then the Logos, was sent as a special messenger of Jehovah to communicate with Abraham and Moses. (Genesis 22:11, 12; Exodus 3:2, 5, 8) At the head of God's organization, possessing all power and authority, and carrying out the divine plan, the Lord Jesus Christ is the Messenger and the Angel of Jehovah. He is the most highly exalted, far above powers and principalities; and he is referred to by the prophet as the Messenger of the covenant.—Mal. 3:1.

[20] Looking down to the time of the inauguration of the New Covenant, which shall result in blessing mankind with life and happiness, the Lord Jesus Christ is referred to by Job as a messenger or angel. "If there be a messenger with him, an interpreter, one among a thousand, to show unto man his uprightness; then he

God's organization, ordained and organized for a purpose. (Colossians 1:18; 1 Peter 2:9, 10) Jesus the Head and his body members constitute the new creation. In the fulness of time every creature who receives the final approval of Jehovah must come under the jurisdiction of Christ Jesus, as it is written: "That in the dispensation of the fulness of times, he might gather together in one all things in Christ, both which are in heaven, and which are on earth; even in him."—Ephesians 1:10; Philippians 2:8, 9.

15 All holy angels are a part of God's organization.

16 The word angel, as used in the Scriptures, means messenger. Whatsoever means the Lord would use to carry out his purpose, it might be properly said that such is an angel of the Lord. An angel may be, therefore, either animate or inanimate; an angel may be either a spirit or a human being. All messengers or angels used by Jehovah may properly be said to be, for the time being at least, a part of his organization. When the Lord used one of his prophets to carry a message to his people, such prophet was then for the time being an angel of the Lord.—Haggai 1:13.

17 The priests of Israel were designated as angels or messengers of the Lord, at whose lips the people should hear and learn the law. (Malachi 2:7) The great Pyramid of Egypt, standing as a silent and inanimate witness of the Lord, is a messenger; and its testimony speaks with great eloquence concerning the divine plan. (Isaiah 19:19, 20) John the Baptist was a messenger of the Lord, therefore an angel sent to perform certain duties.

is gracious unto him, and saith, Deliver him from going down to the pit; I have found a ransom. His flesh shall be fresher than a child's: he shall return to the days of his youth." (Job 33:23-25) Here the exalted Lord and King is spoken of as the Interpreter, who points out to man the way to uprightness. He is gracious to man, delivers him from going down into the tomb, and restores him to perfection of body and mind.

21 The Scriptures show that God's law delivered to Israel was presented by the angels to the mediator. (Acts 7:53; Galatians 3:19; Hebrews 2:2) These, of course, were spirit beings and members of God's organization.

22 By way of comparison and to show how much greater is the Lord Jesus than others as a messenger and angel of Jehovah, the apostle Paul devotes much of his epistle to the Hebrews. The gist of his argument is that Jesus has been appointed heir of all things, and that this inheritance which he has obtained is much more excellent in every way than was that which was appointed to the angels. He is the only one who is the express image of Jehovah. Further, Paul's argument is that when God shall a second time bring the First Begotten into the world, it will be an occasion for all the angels of Jehovah to worship him; that because of his special zeal for righteousness, Jehovah has anointed him above all others of his realm. The Apostle then proceeds to show that as a man Jesus was made a little lower than the angels, in order that he might redeem mankind. As a perfect man he was crowned with glory and honor.—Hebrews 2:9, 10.

NOVEMBER 15, 1928   The WATCH TOWER   341

true, that would be an admission on God's part that his Word needs corroborative proof and is therefore insufficient in itself. If his Word needs corroborative proof, then the statement in the Psalms, that his Word is the guide for his children, could not be true. If his Word is sufficient as a guide for his children, then corroborative proof of his Word is superfluous. God does not do superfluous and unnecessary things. It belittles his written Word to say that it needs corroborative proof. The Scriptures lay down the rule that the man of God is made perfect by knowing and obeying the Word of God. (2 Tim. 3:16, 17; John 17:17) Therefore it was prophetically written for the benefit of the child of God: "Thy word have I hid in mine heart, that I might not sin against thee. I will delight myself in thy statutes: I will not forget thy word. So shall I have wherewith to answer him that reproacheth me: for I trust in thy word. For ever, O Lord, thy word is settled in heaven. Order my steps in thy word: and let not any iniquity have dominion over me. Thy word is very pure: therefore thy servant loveth it. Thy word is true from the beginning: and every one of thy righteous judgments endureth for ever. Let my cry come near before thee, O Lord: give me understanding according to thy word. My tongue shall speak of thy word: for all thy commandments are righteousness."—Ps. 119:11, 16, 42, 89, 133, 140, 160, 169, 172.

13 It was Jehovah who said: "So shall my word be that goeth forth out of my mouth: it shall not return unto me void; but it shall accomplish that which I please, and it shall prosper in the thing whereto I sent it."—Isa. 55:11.

14 The burden is upon the devotees of the pyramid of Gizeh to show from God's Word that he had anything whatsoever to do with the building of that structure of stone. If they make the proof, then they show that the Word of God is insufficient. If they fail to make the proof, then the great pyramid should be put out of the mind of every one who serves God. The facts are, however, that nowhere in the Word of God is the pyramid of Gizeh either directly or indirectly mentioned, as will be seen by examination of the argument that follows.

15 The Scripture says: "Let him that is taught in the word communicate unto him that teacheth in all good things." (Gal. 6:6) If therefore the Word of God does not refer to the pyramid, teaching of and concerning the pyramid, and its measurements, then the drawing of conclusions therefrom is not only contrary to the Scriptures and out of order, but is presumptuous before the Lord. To take a measurement from this visible structure and use that measurement to teach the people of God that such measurement shows that on a day certain God will take his children from earth into heaven is attempting to run

ahead and surely running ahead of the Lord and is therefore presumptuous. He who teaches that which is not found in the Word of God is not teaching "good things".

16 Before the giving of the holy spirit (John 16:13) and for the manifest purpose of establishing the faith of his disciples Jesus caused them to see a vision of transfiguration in the mountain. After the giving of the holy spirit at Pentecost the apostles did not rely upon the evidence furnished by that vision. They looked to and relied upon the Word of God, which they then understood. This proves that all members of the new creation must do likewise and rely upon the Word of God, as it is written: "We have also a more sure word of prophecy; whereunto ye do well that ye take heed, as unto a light that shineth in a dark place, until the day dawn, and the day star arise in your hearts."—2 Pet. 1:19.

17 God has caused his light to shine upon his Word, illuminating it for the guidance of his people. Whatsoever things he caused to be written in his Word are put there for the benefit of the church. (Rom. 15:4) Therefore Paul, instructing those who would be teachers in the church, said: "Holding fast the faithful word, as he hath been taught, that he may be able by sound doctrine both to exhort and to convince the gainsayers." (Titus 1:9) He who relies upon the measurements of the pyramid is not able to "convince the gainsayers", and especially when he produces measurements and attaches important events thereto and these events do not come to pass.

18 Is it not passing strange that if God intended his church to be taught by the measurements of a pile of stone neither Jesus nor any of the apostles has one word to say about it, but, on the contrary, emphasize the necessity of adhering closely to the Word of truth and unselfishly serving it? If, therefore, God did not intend his church to be taught by, of and concerning the great pyramid of Gizeh, then to teach it in the church is a waste of time, to say the least of it. It is more than a waste of time. It is diverting the mind away from the Word of God and from his service.

19 If the pyramid is not mentioned in the Bible, then following its teachings is being led by vain philosophy and false science and not following after Christ. (1 Tim. 6:20; Col. 2:8) If we find that the great pyramid is not mentioned in the Bible, but still insist on holding to it because of so-called scientific measurements, we are treading upon dangerous ground, because we are seeking truth from a source from which God did not command we should seek it. (Ex. 20:5) God has not promised protection to any one who goes outside of his Word for instruction concerning his plan.

The Watchtower, 11/15/28, p. 341

site of the pyramid. If that work was done by human hands or human power, then it must have been done by men who were slaves. That being true, without a doubt many of them died from exhaustion or from being cruelly driven to the task. If there was any sacrifice about that pyramid, it was the sacrifice of slaves to build it. Jehovah God does not accomplish any of his work in that way. The great God of justice and love would not erect a structure which would result in the oppression of slaves and the great loss of life.

¶ 35 It is more reasonable to conclude that the great pyramid of Gizeh, as well as the other pyramids thereabout, also the sphinx, were built by the rulers of Egypt and under the direction of Satan the Devil. The rulers of Egypt are known for their oppression of slaves. The Devil is the great oppressor.

36 Of the sons of Noah that came out of the ark with him Jehovah God chose Shem and blessed him. Abraham was a descendant of Shem, and to Abraham God made promise concerning the carrying out of his plan to bless all the families of the earth. It was to the descendants of Abraham that God gave the Bible, his Word of Truth.

37 Satan the Devil chose Ham, another son of Noah. Egypt is known as the land of Ham. Nimrod was a descendant of Ham, and the Devil exalted Nimrod in the eyes of the people as one greater than Jehovah God. The Devil, by the use of the descendants of Ham, set up Egypt, or the land of Ham, as the first great world power. Then Satan put his knowledge in dead stone, which may be called Satan's Bible, and not God's stone witness. In erecting the pyramid, of course, Satan would put in it some truth, because that is his method of practising fraud and deceit.

38 The information which Lucifer gained at the laying of the foundation of the earth doubtless included much concerning its measurements and God's unit of measurements; and by applying such knowledge Satan could put much in the pyramid that would harmonize with truth and which would serve to deceive men.

39 Based upon astronomical measurements, Professor Smyth concluded that the great pyramid was built in the year 2170 B. C. His conclusion is that at midnight of the autumnal equinox in 2170 B. C. the dragon star, which is a symbol of the Dragon or Devil, shone directly into the entrance of the pyramid of Gizeh; and upon this calculation he fixes the date of its completion. Further (as stated in *Scripture Studies*, Vol. 3, p. 321), using the ascending passage as though it were a telescope, it is claimed that the Pleiades was exactly in line with the ascending passage at the same time and that therefore the ascending passage pointed toward Jehovah. Admitting, for the sake of the argument, that the Pleiades

represents the place of Jehovah's throne, what would these calculations mean? From the entrance passage the dragon star could be seen, but the ascending passage ends in a dead stone and therefore a view of the Pleiades was impossible. It has always been Satan's purpose to exalt himself and to push Jehovah out of sight. (2 Cor. 4: 3, 4) If the above calculations are correct, then such is further corroborative proof that the Devil himself superintended the building of the pyramid of Gizeh.

40 Egypt was the place of great learning. Even Moses was instructed in the learning of the Egyptians. (Acts 7: 22) It was the birthplace of astrology and soothsaying. The astrologers and soothsayers were undoubtedly the instruments of Satan the Devil.

SATAN'S PURPOSE

41 Other pyramids built near Gizeh are undoubtedly the tombs for the dead. It was in Egypt that the embalming of dead bodies had its origin. God had said: "Dust thou art, and unto dust shalt thou return." Manifestly the purpose of embalming dead bodies was to dispute and deny the law of God by keeping the body from moldering and returning to the dust. Of course Satan was the author of that, because it is in exact line with his first lie. Satan would reason something like this: 'It is to be expected that I will receive credit for building these tombs and embalming dead bodies, and the men who reverence God will turn away from them because of me. The pyramid of Gizeh shall not be a tomb, but shall contain many things that will apparently corroborate God's plan, and the men who reverence God will look upon it as the building of God. They will devote much time to the study of this dead stone and try to figure out God's purposes. In doing this they will be going contrary to his plain command. (Ex. 20: 4, 5) Also, I will be turning them away from the Word of God.'

42 Of course no one can tell exactly how Satan reasoned, but the facts show that the above process of reasoning is exactly in line with what has come to pass. Those who have devoted themselves to the pyramid have failed to see some of the most important things that God has revealed for the benefit of his church. The mind of such was turned away from Jehovah and his Word.

43 In another place the prophet says: "Woe to them that go down to Egypt for help." (Isa. 31: 1) Whether we give this text a literal or a symbolic meaning, it is a warning to Israel after the spirit, that is to say, the new creation. If we apply it literally, it means that the new creatures have gone down to literal Egypt to find proof to corroborate God's plan, which is wrong. If we apply it symbolically, it means that new creatures have gone down to the world for help. They have such corroborative proof prophesy lies in my name, saying, I have dreamed, I have dreamed. . . . The prophet that hath a dream, let him tell a dream; and he that hath my word, let him speak my word faithfully. What is the straw to the wheat? saith Jehovah. Is not my word like fire? saith Jehovah; and like a hammer that breaketh the rock in pieces? . . . I am against them that prophesy

lying dreams, . . . yet I sent them not, . . . neither do they profit this people at all, saith Jehovah."

Ezek. 12:24, 25 "There shall be no more any false vision nor flattering divination within the house of Israel. For I am Jehovah; I will speak, and the word that I shall speak shall be performed."

Also: Jer. 14:13-16; Ezek. 13:2, 3, 6, 7; Mic. 3:5-11; Zech. 13:3, 4.

Superior Authorities

DEFINITION

In the field of government there are two parties, (1) the superior, the one who makes the law or rules of action, and (2) the inferior, the one who is bound by the rules of the superior to obey them. For divine government God is the chief superior and man the inferior.

Rom. 13:1-4 "Let every soul be in subjection to the superior authorities ⌈[Jehovah God[1] and Christ Jesus[2]],⌉ for there is no authority except by God [only Christ Jesus and his theocratic organization recognized by God[3]]; the existing authorities [not political governments[4]] stand placed in their relative positions by God [not 'divine right of kings'[5]]. Therefore he who ranges himself up against the authority [Christ Jesus[6]] has taken a stand against the arrangement of God; those who have taken a stand against it will receive judgment to themselves [annihilation from Christ Jesus[7]]."

Jehovah God Is Supreme Above All Superiors[1]

Ps. 62:11, *Mo* "There is one thing God has said; ay, twice have I heard him say it: that power belongs to God."

Job 37:23, *Mo* "The Almighty is beyond our minds. Supreme in power and rich in justice, he violates no right."

Isa. 40:14, 15 "Who hath directed the spirit of Jehovah, or being his counsellor hath taught him? Behold, the nations are as a drop of a bucket, and are accounted as the small dust of the balance: behold, he taketh up the isles as a very little thing."

Rom. 9:20, 21 "O man, who, then, really are you to be answering back to God? Shall the thing molded say to him that

molded it, 'Why did you make me this way?' What? Does not the potter have authority over the clay to make from the same lump one vessel for an honorable use, another for a dishonorable use?"

Heb. 12:9 "Furthermore, we used to have fathers who were of our flesh to discipline us and we used to give them respect. Shall we not much more subject ourselves to the Father of our spiritual life and live?"

Isa. 33:22 "For Jehovah is our judge, Jehovah is our lawgiver, Jehovah is our king; he will save us."

Christ Jesus Is a Superior Second Only to Jehovah[2]

John 17:1, 2 "Jesus spoke these things, and, raising his eyes to

Reorganizing
for Active
Service

JOHN: ⌐When the Society began to be freed for further preaching work following World War I, they soon realized they had been held in spiritual bondage too in many ways. There were many false doctrines and practices that had not yet been cleaned out of the organization.⌐Not all of them were recognized at once, but gradually over the years that followed it became evident to what extent the brothers had been in Babylonish captivity at that time. ⌐With considerable misunderstanding they had accepted earthly political governments as the "superior authorities" that God had ordained according to Romans 13:1; and as a result the Witnesses had been held in fear of man, particularly the civil rulers.⌐

Besides, many were putting emphasis on so-called "character development," in the belief that there were certain saving qualities in their self-merit,[b] and there was considerable creature worship in the organization.[c] Furthermore, such pagan holidays as Christmas were being celebrated,[d] and even the symbol of the cross was used as a sign of Christian devotion.[e] Also, although the name Jehovah was used from

time to time, it was held in the background and its true significance not brought to light. Organizationally the Witnesses were still practicing the democratic style of local congregation government.[f] In other words, it was a time of everyone's doing what was considered right in his own eyes, and the entire arrangement was a loose association without theocratic direction. The change-over in thinking had been so striking in many ways, from the 1870's down to 1918, that these tainted bonds of false conceptions and practices, inherited from the pagan traditions adopted by Christendom, had slipped by unnoticed by the brothers.

Now from the year 1919 a glorious new outlook presented itself. These dedicated servants began to recognize their mistakes and make a public confession of their wrongdoing in their effort to seek Jehovah's forgiveness and be restored to his favor, which they realized had temporarily been lost. They repented of their former course, expressed the desire to change their ways and prayed for Jehovah's forgiveness. They recognized a compromise had been made by cutting out pages 247-253 of *The Finished Mystery* in order to please those who had assumed the position of censor.[g] Another compromise was made as revealed in *The Watch Tower* of June 1, 1918.

a *Studies in the Scriptures*, Vol. I (1886), p. 250 (1926 Ed.). b *W* 1916, pp. 155-157; *W* 1926, pp. 131-137. c *W* 1916, pp. 356-370. d *W* 1919, p. 31; *W* 1946, p. 361. e *W* 1906, p. 274. f *W* 1913, p. 381. g *W* 1918, p. 77.

of Bread, not as Bread Providers, or as coming themselves out of the House of Bread—for they themselves first had to take of the living Bread—are his faithful footstep followers, the "called and chosen and faithful," who, with him, constitute God's capital organization that rules over his universal organization.—Rev. 17: 14; 14:1, 3.

Of course, if Jesus Christ had been made Ruler without coming from this heavenly House of Bread, without his first having ransomed mankind and presented the merit of his sacrifice in heaven, he could not give everlasting life to mankind, regardless of how able and beneficent his rule might be. On the other hand, without his being sent forth as the Ruler, he could not give mankind the benefit of his

being the Bread of life in the House of Bread.

How much all of us are indebted to this Ruler out of the House of Bread! What a fine example he set for all his followers! Dedicated Christians who appreciate the benefits that are and will yet be theirs and the example he set will delight to serve him. They will do as he did when upon earth, go about "preaching and declaring the good news of the kingdom of God." (Luke 8:1) And as he trained others, so these will also do. For many, January will be a long, cold month, but what are the discomforts of inclement weather compared with the joys that come from being in the direct service of the Ruler out of the House of Bread, bringing the Bread of life to deserving hungry and dying ones!

DO YOU REMEMBER?

Have you read the recent issues of *The Watchtower* carefully? If so, you should recognize these important points. Check yourself.
● Why is it not safe for Christians to follow men?

Because men are imperfect, make mistakes and at times prove unfaithful. However, so long as they are of "those who through faith and patience inherited the promises" they may be imitated.—P. 535.*
● What light do the Psalms throw on life's roadway?

They contain accurate history, inspired prophecy, sound doctrine and admonition to right conduct.—Pp. 550, 551.
● Why cannot 1 John 5:7 be used to prove the trinity teaching?

Because it is spurious, not genuine; it being added later.—P. 556.
● Did the apostle John borrow from Plato his teaching regarding Jesus' being the Word?

No, he did not. He termed Jesus the Word because the Bible shows that the prehuman Jesus was God's spokesman.—Pp. 602, 603.
● Is extrasensory perception for Christians?

No; for its manifestations, such as clairvoyance, telepathy, visions, object readings and prediction indicate spiritism.—Pp. 647, 648.
● What is relative subjection?

It is a subjection related to something else;

specifically, a subjection limited or qualified by God's will.—P. 651.
● Who is the "king" mentioned at 1 Peter 2:17, for whom Christians are to have honor?

Any king or any political ruler having governors under him.—Pp. 659, 660.
● What is the "human creation" to which Christians are to subject themselves?

A ruling office created by humans of this world or the one occupying such an office. —P. 660.
● To whom is "relative subjection" due?

It is due to husbands, parents, masters of slaves and political governments.—Pp. 665, 666.
● Who are the "superior authorities" to whom Christians are to be in subjection?

The duly constituted political governments of this world.—Pp. 684, 685.
● In what way are the "superior authorities" God's ministers?

In that they punish wrongdoers.—P. 712.
● For what compelling reason should Christians be in subjection to the "superior authorities"?

For conscience' sake.—Pp. 714, 715.
● Why is faith termed "the evident demonstration of realities though not beheld"?

Because it makes evident what has not been discerned before and at the same time refutes what appears to be the case but is not.—P. 751.

* All references are to *The Watchtower* for 1962.

trine of the Trinity ('God in three persons'), the immortality of the human soul, a hellfire of torment for the wicked, and other unscriptural teachings. They say that the Witnesses *deceived* them, sometimes for many years—the same charge that "false apostles" made against Paul. But now, they say, they have suddenly seen the light—that these doctrines that they had rejected were true all along. They repent at having doubted such doctrines and having talked against these while being associated with the Witnesses.

Does not this wavering from one position to another raise questions as to the sincerity of these opposers? Most of them were former church members who came to declare that such doctrines were false, originating in non-Christian religions. While they were associated with Jehovah's Witnesses they offered proofs of their conviction to others as they preached to them. Are these men, when turning against Jehovah's Witnesses, following the pattern of the apostle Paul? He once was a firm believer in Judaism, believing that he could gain righteousness by works of the Mosaic law. But he threw these things down when he became a Christian. His opposers said that Christians should return to subjection to the things of the Law, and trust in such works for salvation. Paul answered: "If the very things that I once threw down I build up again, I demonstrate myself to be a *transgressor*."—Gal. 2:18.

It is a serious matter to represent God and Christ in one way, then find that our understanding of the major teachings and fundamental doctrines of the Scriptures was in error, and then after that, to go back to the very doctrines that, by years of study, we had thoroughly determined to be in error. Christians cannot be vacillating—'wishy-washy'—about such fundamental teachings. What confidence can one put in the sincerity or judgment of such persons?

Moreover, Jesus said of his disciples: "They are no part of the world." (John 17:16) But who can deny that the churches of Christendom are an integral part of the world? Those going back to ally themselves with these churches ignore the fact that the clergy have blessed the wars of the nations, members of the same denomination praying on both sides for the victory of their own army and the destruction of the other. Persons returning to support these denominations bring back upon themselves the bloodguilt from which they were once freed.—Compare Numbers 35:33; Revelation 18:24.

If a person has cleaned up from doctrines that dishonor God—the Trinity, the fiendish torment of souls in an eternal hell of fire, the destruction of our planet Earth, the support of blood-spilling national warfare and like beliefs that would make the Christian defiled as a part of the world—and then turns back to take up these doctrines again, he is doing what the apostle Peter described of some persons in his day. Peter wrote: "Certainly if, after having escaped from the defilements of the world by an accurate knowledge of the Lord and Savior Jesus Christ, they get involved again with these very things and are overcome, the final conditions have become worse for them than the first. For it would have been better for them not to have accurately known the path of righteousness than after knowing it accurately to turn away from the holy commandment delivered to them. The saying of the true proverb has happened to them: 'The dog has returned to its own vomit, and the sow that was bathed to rolling in the mire.'"—2 Pet. 2:20-22.

MAKING SURE OF ONE'S POSITION

How, then, can a person be sure that his position is right if he has developed faith in Jehovah God and His kingdom through studying with Jehovah's Witness-

The Watchtower, 5/15/76, p. 298

Once more we read: "Jesus Christ, by the grace of God, tasted death for every man." How, Lord? we ask, If he tasted death for the one hundred and forty-three billions, and from other causes it becomes efficacious only to one billion, is not his death comparatively a failure?

Again: "Behold I bring you glad tidings of great joy, which shall be to *all people*." Surely it is to but a little flock to whom it has been glad tidings, and not to *all people*.

Another is: "There is one God, and one Mediator between God and man, Christ Jesus, who gave himself a ransom for all." A ransom, then why should not *all* have *some benefit* from Christ's death?

Oh, how dark, how inconsistent do these statements appear when we remember that the Gospel Church is "a little flock." Oh, how we wish it would please God to open our eyes that we might understand the Scriptures, for we feel sure that did we but understand, it must all seem clear, it must all declare in thunder tone, "God is Love." Oh, that we had the key! Do you want it?—Are you sure you do? It is the last text we quoted, "Who gave himself a ransom for all, *to be testified in due time.*" Due time. Ah, now we see. God has a due time for everything. He could have testified it to this one hundred and forty-two billions in their life time. Then that would have been their due time; as it was not so, their due time must be future. We know that now is our due time, because it is testified to us now. Christ was a ransom for you before you were born, but it was not due time for you to hear it until years after. So with the Hottentot; Christ was his ransom and at the same time was yours; he has not heard it yet, and may not in this life; but in God's *due* time he will.

But does not death end probation? one inquires. There is no scripture which says so, we answer, and all the above and many more scriptures would be meaningless or worse,

IF DEATH ENDS ALL

to the ignorant masses of the world. The only scripture ever quoted to prove this generally entertained view, is, "As the tree falleth, so it lies." If this has *any* relation to man and his future, it indicates that in whatever condition of knowledge or ignorance he enters death, he remains the same until he is raised up again.

But can knowledge ever reach these billions in their graves while dead? No; God has provided for the resurrection of

mouth of all the holy prophets." They do all teach it. Ezekiel tells us of the whole house of the valley of dry bones, "This is the whole house of Israel;" and God says to them, "I will bring you up out of your graves, and bring you into your own land." This agrees with St. Paul, Rom. vi. 25, 26. Blindness in part is happened to Israel until the fullness of the Gentiles (the Gospel Church, the elect company "taken out of the Gentiles") be come in, and so all Israel shall be saved, or brought back from their cast-off condition. For "God hath not cast off His people whom He foreknew." They were cut off from His favor while the *bride of Christ* was being selected, but will return to favor when that work is accomplished.—Vs. 28 to 33. The prophets are full of statements of how God will "plant them again, and they shall be no more plucked up." This does not refer to restorations from former captivities in Babylon, Syria, &c., for the Lord says, "*In that day* it shall no more be a proverb among you 'the fathers ate a sour grape and the children's teeth are set on edge;' but every man shall die for his own sin." This is not the case now. You do not die for your own sin, but for Adam's.—"As in Adam all die." He ate the sour grape, and our forefathers continued to eat them, entailing further sickness and misery upon us. The day in which "every man shall die *for his own sin*," is this Millennial or Restitution day. But when restored to the same conditions as Adam, will they not be as liable to sin and fall again as he was? No; they will be liable, but not *as liable*; they have learned in their time the lesson which God designed to teach to all, viz., "The exceeding sinfulness of sin." They will be prepared to appreciate the good and shun the evil, and the Gospel Church then glorified will be, "the kings (rulers) and priests" (teachers) of that new age, for "Unto the angels hath He not put in subjection the word (age) to come, whereof we speak," &c. Then through "the second Adam" and His helpmeet they may be begotten into their spiritual likeness.

But are we sure that God intends these blessings for any but the "people whom He foreknew" (the Jews)? Yes. He mentions other nations also by name, and speaks of their restitution. Let me give you *an illustration that will be forcible:*

THE SODOMITES.

Surely if we find *their* restitution mentioned you will be satisfied. But why should they not have an opportunity to obtain eternal life as well as you or the Jew? They were not wicked them all. For "as in Adam *all* die, even so in Christ shall *all* be made alive." As death came by the first Adam, so life comes by the second Adam. Everything that mankind lost in the first, is to be restored in the second. Hence, the age following Christ's second coming is spoken of as "the times of restitution."

Life is one of the things lost, and is to be one of the things restored. Mark me! I do not say eternal life is given them. No; Adam never had eternal life to lose; if he had it, he could not have died. He had natural life, lost natural life, and it is to be natural life that the second Adam restores. This is a certain sort of *salvation* that Christ accomplishes for all; but the *eternal* salvation, which believers receive, is entirely different. This enables us to use another text, which is little used except by Universalists, and although not Universalists, yet we claim the right to use all Scripture. It reads: "We trust in the living God, who is the Saviour of all men, especially of them which believe." All men are saved or rescued from the loss entailed on them through Adam, by having all those lost things, including natural life, restored to them. He is also the "especial Saviour of them which believe." For believers who now constitute the body of Christ are the happy recipients of the gift of God, *eternal* life. While those of the *world* are raised *natural* bodies, those of the *Church* are raised *spiritual* bodies, "neither can *they* die any more, but are like the angels of God,"

Now we see that "the testimony in *due* time" explains all of those troublous texts. In due time it shall be "glad tidings of great joy to all people." In due time that "True Light shall lighten every man that cometh into the world," and in no other way can these scriptures be used without wresting. We take them to mean just what they say. Paul carries out the line of argument with emphasis in Rom. v. 18, 19. He reasons that as all men were condemned to death and suffered it because of Adam's transgression, so also Christ's righteousness justifies *all* to life again. All lost life, not of our own will or choice, in the first Adam; all receive life at the hands of the second Adam, **equally** without their will or choice.

When thus brought to life, and the love of God testified to them, their probation,

THEIR FIRST CHANCE,

begins, for we do not preach a *second chance* for any.
But Peter tells us, that "the restitution is spoken of by the

in the proper sense, for they did not have law or much knowledge. True, they were not righteous, but neither were you when God gave you your opportunity. Christ's own words shall tell us that they are *not as guilty* in His sight as the Jews, who had more knowledge: "Woe unto thee, Capernaum, for if the mighty works which have been done in thee had been done in Sodom it would have remained unto this day." Thus Christ's own words teach us that they had not had their full opportunity. "Remember," Christ says of the Sodomites, that "God rained down fire and *destroyed them all.*" So, if their restoration is spoken of, it *implies* their resurrection.

Let us look at the prophecy, Ezek. xvi. 48 to the close. Read it carefully. God here speaks of Israel and compares her with her neighbor, Samaria, and also with the *Sodomites*, whom He says, "I took away as I saw good." Why did God see good to take away these people without giving them a chance of eternal life through the knowledge of "the only name?" Because it was not their *due time.* They will come to a knowledge of the truth when *restored.* ¶ He'll save them from death's bondage first, and then give them knowledge. As it is written: "God will have *all men to be saved,* and to come to a *knowledge of the truth.*" When brought to the knowledge, then, and not until then, are they on trial for *eternal* life. With this thought, and with no other, can we understand the dealings of the God of love with those Amalekites and other nations, whom He not only permitted, but commanded Israel to butcher. "Slay Amalek utterly—leave neither man, woman or child." "Spare not the little ones." How often my heart has ached, and yours, too, as we sought to reconcile this apparent wantonness on God's part with the teachings of the new dispensation. "God is love," "Love your enemies," &c. Now we can see that the entire Jewish age was a type of the higher, Gospel age; Israel's victories and conquests merely pictures of the Christian's battles with sin, etc. These Amalekites and Sodomites and others were used to illustrate, or to be "examples" "for our admonition;" and these people might just as well die so, as of disease and plague, and it mattered little to them as they were merely learning to know *evil,* that when on trial, "*in due time,*" they might learn *good* and be able to discriminate and choose life.

But let us read the prophecy further. After comparing Israel with Sodom and Samaria, and pronouncing her worse, v. 53 says: "When I bring again the captivity [in death, all

[7]

338   𝔗𝔥𝔢 WATCHTOWER   BROOKLYN, N. Y.

discussing restoration of the theocratic organization, not resurrection.

JUDGMENT UPON ISRAEL IN JESUS' DAY

15 Another judgment period is brought into view when those championing resurrection for exterminated Sodomites quote Jesus' words on a certain occasion. He had reproached the unrepentant Jewish cities of Chorazin and Bethsaida, which had witnessed many of his powerful works, then said: "And you, Capernaum, will you perhaps be exalted to heaven? Down to Hades you will come; because if the powerful works that took place in you had taken place in Sodom, it would have remained until this very day. Consequently I say to you people, It will be more endurable for the land of Sodom on Judgment Day than for you." (Matt. 10:14, 15; 11:20-24; Luke 10:10-15, NW) From this some argue that there is a future judgment, in the millennial reign, for both Sodom and these Jewish cities.

16 If we take this expression to mean that, then it would contradict Jude's statement that Sodom had already undergone the "judicial punishment of everlasting fire". Actually, Jesus was using a form of speech construction common in Biblical times. He used a similar construction when he said: "It is easier, in fact, for a camel to get through the eye of a sewing needle than for a rich man to get into the kingdom of God." (Luke 18:25, NW) No sane person would believe a camel could squeeze through a needle's eye. Yet if this obviously impossible thing were said to be easier than something else, would that not powerfully emphasize the utter impossibility of the other thing? So Jesus forcefully made the point that rich ones loath to part with their wealth would not enter the kingdom.

Similarly, Sodom did not endure its judgment day, had failed completely, and the Jews knew its fate was sealed. Their opinion of Sodom was the lowest possible. So when Jesus told them that it would be more endurable for utterly depraved Sodom than for these Jewish cities they got the powerful point.

17 These Jewish cities had heard the warning and had seen powerful works; they had had their fair judgment trial and by their decision showed they were worthy of eternal destruction. (Matt. 10:5-15; Luke 10:8-12; John 12:37, NW) By witnessing miraculous cures performed by the power of the holy spirit and yet refusing to accept the message, the inhabitants of these cities were sinning against the holy spirit, which is the unforgivable sin meriting second death. They ranged themselves alongside the Pharisees who saw Jesus heal a demon-possessed man, but refused to accept this manifest operation of the holy spirit. Because of this Jesus told them they would never have forgiveness, neither in the present system of things nor in the next, the new world. Being judged adversely, unforgivable in both the old world and the new world, it would be useless to resurrect them in the millennium. Jesus pronounced judgment against them: "Serpents, offspring of vipers, how are you to flee from the judgment of Gehenna?" If the blind religious leaders were to land there, so were their blind Jewish followers. And when the false religious leaders converted some heathen they did not bring him into the true worship that would cleanse him of his past sins against God, but merely added to his past sins the religious sinfulness and hypocrisy which they taught him, doubling his burden of guilt. Thus the proselyte became twice as much a "subject for Gehenna" as the scribes and

---

15. Why do some argue for a future judgment for both Sodom and the Jews of Jesus' day?
16. What did Jesus mean when he said judgment would be more endurable for Sodom than certain Jewish cities?

17. Why would it be useless to resurrect the Jewish clergy, their Jewish followers, and their Gentile converts?

Questions from Readers

● Since Jude 7 shows that Sodom and Gomorrah became a "warning example by undergoing the judicial punishment of everlasting fire," does that not bar the inhabitants of those cities from a resurrection?—A.C., U.S.A.

Reading only that verse, without our taking into consideration what the rest of the Bible has to say on the matter, one might draw such a conclusion. But other scriptures present additional facts that cannot be ignored if we are going to arrive at a sound conclusion.

For example, at Matthew 11:23 it is written: "If the powerful works that took place in [Capernaum] had taken place in Sodom, it would have remained until this very day." Obviously, this does not mean that the same individuals who were living in Sodom at the time of its destruction would have remained alive for over 1900 years down to the time when Jesus spoke those words, but that the city would have remained as an inhabited place.

Then the next verse refers to the Judgment Day, saying: "Consequently I say to you people, It will be more endurable for the land of Sodom on Judgment Day than for you." (Matt. 11:24) Similarly, at Matthew 10:15 are recorded Jesus' words: "Truly I say to you, It will be more endurable for the land of Sodom and Gomorrah on Judgment Day than for that city" where the people would reject the message carried by Jesus' disciples. For it to be "more endurable for the land of Sodom and Gomorrah" than for others, it would be necessary for former inhabitants of that land to be present on Judgment Day. It is not the literal land, the ground, that is to be judged. Revelation chapter 20 shows that it will be persons raised from the dead who will stand "before the throne." Nor will judgment be passed on them as groups, as former inhabitants of certain lands, but they will be "judged individually according to their deeds" during the time of judgment. So apparently individuals who used to live in that land will be resurrected.—Rev. 20:12, 13.

What is it, then, that underwent "the judicial punishment of everlasting fire"? While the inhabitants of the cities were certainly destroyed, apparently it was not the people but the *cities themselves* that were everlastingly destroyed. They have not been rebuilt down to this day. Notably, J. Penrose Harland wrote: "It has been shown that Sodom, Gomorrah, Admah, and Zeboiim were doubtless situated in the area now covered by the waters of the southern part of the Dead Sea."—*The Biblical Archaeologist Reader* (1961), page 59; see also Isaiah 13:19, 20.

What happened to the inhabitants of Sodom and Gomorrah at the time that Jehovah rained fire and sulphur on them from heaven stands as a warning to all to avoid immoral conduct such as was carried on in those cities.

● On what animal did Jesus Christ make his triumphal ride into Jerusalem? Matthew 21:7 mentions both an ass and a colt.—M.E., U.S.A.

Jesus said to the disciples he sent into Jerusalem: "You will at once find an ass tied, and a colt with her." (Matt. 21:2) So there was a mother or she-ass and a colt that was yet with its mother. Then at Matthew 21:7 we read: "They brought the ass and its colt, and they put upon these their outer garments, and he seated himself upon them."

We will be aided to understand which animal Jesus actually used if we first read the prophecy that Jesus was thus fulfilling. Translated directly from Hebrew, Zechariah 9:9 reads: "Be very joyful, O daughter of Zion. Shout in triumph, O daughter of Jerusalem. Look! Your king himself comes to you. He is righteous, yes, saved; humble, and riding upon an ass, even upon a full-grown animal the son of a she-ass." Thus, the Messiah would use a "full-grown" male animal, "the son of a she-ass."

The accounts in Mark, Luke and John mention only that one animal, the one Jesus rode. They refer to it both as an "ass" and as a "colt." Obviously, that animal could be identified satisfactorily by either term. (Mark 11:2-7; Luke 19:30-35; John 12:14, 15) Interestingly, both Mark and Luke show that the "colt" was one "on which none of mankind [had] yet sat." While it was a mature male animal, it had not yet been separated from its mother and used as a mount. So the disciples brought both the she-ass and its colt to Jesus, but the one he rode was the male ass, the colt.

We are informed that the disciples "put upon these their outer garments, and [Jesus] seated himself upon them." Thus Jesus seated himself, not on both the she-ass and its colt, but on the outer garments placed on the colt. Then Christ rode into Jerusalem.

spoken of (1) Israelites destroyed for lack of faith, and (2) angels who sinned and are 'reserved with eternal bonds for the judgment of the great day.' Then Jude wrote: "So too Sodom and Gomorrah . . . are placed before us as a warning example by undergoing the judicial punishment of everlasting fire." This text has been applied to the actual cities' being destroyed everlastingly, not the people. However, in view of Jude 5 and 6, likely most people would take verse 7 to mean a judicial punishment of individuals. (Similarly, Matthew 11:20-24 would be understood as criticizing people, not stones or buildings.) In this light, Jude 7 would mean that the wicked people of Sodom/Gomorrah were judged and destroyed everlastingly.*

Looking elsewhere, we find it noteworthy that more than once the Bible links the Flood and Sodom/Gomorrah. In what context?

When asked about "the conclusion of the system of things," Je-

tion. Jesus added: "The same way it will be on that day when the Son of man is to be revealed." (Luke 17:26-30; compare Matthew 24: 36-39.) Was Jesus illustrating just an attitude, or does the context in which he used these examples suggest that eternal judgments were involved?

Later, Peter wrote about God's judgments and His punishing those deserving it. Then Peter used three examples: The angels that sinned, the ancient world of Noah's time, and those destroyed in Sodom/Gomorrah. The latter, Peter said, 'set a pattern for ungodly persons of things to come.' (2 Peter 2:4-9) Thereafter, he

us at the revelation of the Lord Jesus from heaven with his powerful angels in a flaming fire, as he brings vengeance upon those who do not know God and those who do not obey the good news about our Lord Jesus. These very ones will undergo the judicial punishment of everlasting destruction from before the Lord and from the glory of his strength."

There is an interesting similarity in phraseology between this description and what Jude said occurred in the case of Sodom. Furthermore, Matthew 25:31-46 and Revelation 19:11-21 indicate that "the goats" cut off in the coming war of God will experience "eversus foretold the coming "end" and a "great tribulation such as has not occurred since the world's beginning." (Matthew 24:3, 14, 21) He went on to speak of "the days of Noah" and what "occurred in the days of Lot" as being examples of people who took no note of warning about coming destruc-

* At Ezekiel 16:53-55, "Sodom and her dependent towns" are mentioned, not in connection with the resurrection, but figuratively with regard to Jerusalem and her daughters. (Compare Revelation 11:8.) See also *The Watchtower*, June 1, 1952, page 337.

compared the destruction that people suffered in the Deluge with the coming "day of judgment and of destruction of the ungodly men." That precedes the promised new heavens and new earth. —2 Peter 3:5-13.

Likewise, at the end of the present wicked system, will those whom God executes have had a final judgment? That is the indication of 2 Thessalonians 1:6-9: "It is righteous on God's part to repay tribulation to those who make tribulation for you, but, to you who suffer tribulation, relief along with

lasting cutting-off" in "the lake of fire," which symbolizes permanent annihilation.* —Revelation 20:10, 14.

Consequently, in addition to what Jude 7 says, the Bible uses Sodom/Gomorrah and the Flood as patterns for the destructive end of the present wicked system. It is apparent, then, that those whom God executed in those past judgments experienced irreversible destruction. Of course, each of us can confirm that by his proving faithful to Jehovah now. In that way we will qualify to be alive in the new world to see whom he resurrects and whom he does not. We know that his judgments are perfect. Elihu assured us: "For a fact, God himself does not act wickedly, and the Almighty himself does not pervert judgment." —Job 34:10, 12.

* Compare "Questions From Readers" in *The Watchtower* of August 1, 1979.

9

Doctoring Medical Doctrines

Although the doctrinal flip-flops outlined in our previous chapter may have adversely affected the spiritual or emotional health of some Jehovah's Witnesses who lived through the changes and were confused by them, other alterations in Watchtower teaching have caused followers severe physical problems, even death.

An obvious example, of course, is the refusal of blood transfusions, introduced as a requirement in the mid-1940s and since then become a trademark of Jehovah's Witnesses. But before examining that teaching, we do well to look further back at the sect's earlier statements on medical matters.

Back in 1913, the July 1 issue of *The Watch Tower* carried this notice on page 200:

A Cure for Surface Cancer

. . . We have recently learned of a very effective and simple remedy for cancers which show themselves on the surface of the body. We are informed that a physician, after testing this remedy, paid $1000 for the information, and that he has established a Cancer Hospital which is doing good work. The recipe has come to us free and we are willing to communicate the formula, but only to those who are troubled with surface cancers and who will write to us directly, stating particulars. No fee will be charged, but in order to protect the sufferers, we require a promise that they will not sell the formula to others, nor receive pay for the use of it, nor communicate the formula to anybody. Any one known to be a sufferer can be informed of the terms on which the prescription is obtainable through us [see p. 107].

Unfortunately, we have no documentation as to just what this so-called cure consisted of, or how many readers wrote in for it. But it is clear as we look back from the end of the twentieth century that a real cure for cancer was not introduced to mankind by the Watchtower Society in 1913.

Eighteen years later an article in the Society's *Golden Age* magazine (later renamed *Consolation* and today called *Awake!*) stated, "Vaccination is a direct violation of the everlasting covenant that God made with Noah after the flood" (2/4/31, p. 293 [see p. 108]). From then on, followers were deadly serious about avoiding vaccination. An elderly Jehovah's Witness outlined for me what parents she knew did in situations where a vaccination was legally required for admission of their children to school. The child would be taken to a Witness doctor or other cooperating medical professional who would use acid to burn a "vaccination" mark on the child's arm. If more "proof" were needed, phony documents could also be prepared to supplement the mark on the arm.

After teaching the doctrine as "God's law" for some twenty years, the Watchtower Society quietly dropped it in the early 1950s. Since then, the children of Jehovah's Witnesses have been freely vaccinated. In fact any Witness today who presented false evidence of vaccination to his or her child's public school authorities would risk discipline from a congregation judicial committee.

Another new medical doctrine was born in 1967, when *The Watchtower* banned organ transplants, calling them "cannibalism":

> Those who submit to such operations are thus living off the flesh of another human. That is cannibalistic. However, in allowing man to eat animal flesh Jehovah God did not grant permission for humans to try to perpetuate their lives by cannibalistically taking into their bodies human flesh, whether chewed or in the form of whole organs or body parts taken from others (*The Watchtower*, 11/15/67, p. 702 [see p. 109]).

The *Awake!* magazine of June 8, 1968, further amplified on this, saying:

> There are those, such as the Christian witnesses of Jehovah, who consider *all* transplants between humans as cannibalism. . . (p. 21 [*see* p. 110]).

From then on JWs who required a cornea transplant to retain their eyesight had to refuse the procedure. (A former elder in England once wrote telling me that he resigned after seeing a woman in his congregation go blind, in obedience to this command.) Likewise one who needed a kidney transplant to stay alive had to spurn that life-saving procedure also.

But the horror of it all became apparent in 1980, when the Watchtower Society again reversed itself and lifted its ban on organ transplants. No longer would a JW who received a kidney or a cornea face the punishment of disfellowshiping. Instead, *The Watchtower* said:

> . . . there is no Biblical command pointedly forbidding the taking in of other human tissue. . . . It is a matter for personal decision. (Gal. 6:5) The congregation judicial committee would not take disciplinary action if someone accepted an organ transplant. . .3/15/80, p. 31 [*see* p. 111]).

No apology was given for those who lost their sight, their health or their life by following the organization's previous instructions in the years between 1967 and 1980.

The ban on blood transfusions has been in force from the mid-1940s until now. Based on the Watchtower Society's unique interpretation of Jewish dietary laws that prohibited "eating" blood, the organization forbids Witnesses to accept a transfusion even when life is at stake. Interestingly, Leviticus 3:17 commands the nation of ancient Israel, "that ye eat neither fat nor blood" (KJV). The Society generally ignores the reference to fat, allowing followers to eat fat if they wish. But the reference to "eating" blood is broadened to include medical transfusions. Virtually no one else understands it that way; even orthodox Jews, to whom the law was originally given and who meticulously drain blood from their kosher food, will accept a transfusion.

When discussing this with your JW loved one you might say something like this: "Of course, each individual must follow his or her own conscience in this matter. But, given the Watchtower's track record of prohibiting vaccinations for over twenty years, then reversing itself, and later banning organ transplants for thirteen years before again changing the interpretation, one can only wonder how long it will be until the Society reinterprets the Bible verses it now uses to forbid transfusions. Remembering those who suffered or died for lack of a vaccination or transplant, only to see those teachings later abandoned, it would seem a poor risk to trust one's life to the Watchtower's present interpretation on transfusions."

In discussing the documents presented here, you could use tactful questions to help your JW loved one draw an even broader conclusion: an organization whose changing doctrines damage physical health could hardly be relied upon to keep you spiritually healthy.

But be sure *not* to end the conversation by asking whether he or she is now willing to receive a transfusion. That would be forcing the issue. It may take some time for all of this information to sink in and for the individual to rethink the matter. Remember, too, that your purpose is not to change his or her mind on transfusions; that would be failing to see the forest for the trees. The target of the documentation and discussions outlined in each of these chapters is *the Watchtower organization itself*—to prove that it is not what it claims to be. Its long history of misleading followers in the area of medical treatment is just one more piece of evidence pointing to that conclusion.

therefore, be content to elaborate a little his view of the fifth of these trials belonging to this harvest time, and written for our admonition, as "our types."

THE "VOW," REPRESENTED IN THE TASSELS

In Numbers 16, we have in great detail the fifth of "these things written for our admonition," as "our types." Our brother urges that the account really begins with the last four verses of Numbers 15. There the Lord directed Moses, saying, "Speak unto the children of Israel, and bid them that they make them fringes in the borders of their garments, throughout their generations, and that they put upon the fringe of the borders a riband of blue. And it shall be unto you for a fringe, that ye may look upon it, and remember all the commandments of the Lord, and do them; and that ye seek not after your own heart, and your own eyes, after which ye use to go a whoring; that ye may remember and do all my commandments, and be holy unto your God."—Num. 15:38-40.

The brother points out that the word here rendered ... is in the Hebrew *tsitsith*, and signifies a ... still follow this command. Next to ... a few inches long ...

... not after ... ... the vow is a sugges-... ... commandments and speak not after our own heart of the flesh, nor after our own wisdom, but that we remember and do all of God's will and requirements and glorify our God. The rising of Korah, Dathan, Abiram and On, with the two hundred and fifty of the princepal men of the congregation, represented in type the opposition engendered against the Lord's harvest work, now being carried on through this journal and the Watch Tower Society, and which took for its text, in opposition to the Vow suggested, "Ye take too much upon you, seeing all the congregation are holy, every one of them." Wherefore then lift ye up so high a standard of the Lord? Why lift up so high a standard of righteous endeavor of thought and word and deed?

MOSES EXPOSTULATED IN VAIN

How Moses entreated and expostulated, and how he was reviled, is described in Numbers 16:4-35, also the final result—that Korah, Dathan, Abiram and their families were swallowed up by the opening of the earth, and the band of two hundred and fifty were destroyed by fire. This is interpreted to signify that those rebellious ones who posed as being so holy were disapproved of the Lord, and in some manner, in the antitype, will lose their spiritual life—possibly by being swallowed up, or consumed, by worldliness, business, etc. Our interpreter suggests that this taking of censers and offering of incense by these men, pictures the bringing forth of many tracts and pamphlets as offerings of incense to God by those who oppose us.

Aaron stood in the midst of the offerers with his censer ... incense, and his offering alone was accepted. The brother ... attention to the sequel of the matter, which he ... degree be future.

... ad of recognizing the ... over ... and teachers. ... yourselves therefore ... may exalt you in due time."

Another lesson is that loyalty to God means that we shall remember that he has undertaken the supervision of his church's affairs, and that he is competent for all that he has undertaken. Consequently, the loyal and obedient must be careful how they undertake to be or to do, to make or to break, anything connected with the work of the Lord. They are more and more to expect and look for divine leadings in all of their affairs, and equally in the affairs of the church of Christ.

A CURE FOR SURFACE CANCER

Cancer troubles are becoming more numerous. We know of no remedy for internal cancers except surgery. Even then a cure is doubtful. We have recently learned of a very effective and simple remedy for cancers which show themselves on the surface of the body. We are informed that a physician, after testing this remedy, paid $1,000 for the information, and that he has established a Cancer Hospital which is doing good work. The recipe has come to us free and we are willing to communicate the formula, but to those only who are troubled with surface cancers and who will write to us directly, stating particulars. No fee will be charged, but in order to protect the sufferers, we require a promise that they will not sell the formula to others, nor receive pay for the use of it, nor communicate the formula to anybody. Any one known to be a sufferer can be informed of the terms on which the prescription is obtainable through us.

[5268]

The Watchtower, 7/1/13, p. 200

FEBRUARY 4, 1931   The GOLDEN AGE   293

on the earth as water. Thou shalt not eat it; that it may go well with thee, and with thy children after thee, when thou shalt do that which is right in the sight of the Lord.

What About Armageddon?

When we see these scriptures, and note the emphasis with which these commands not to mingle human blood and animal blood are repeated over and over, we can but wonder what part the violation, the general and impudent violation, of the spirit of this command will play in the battle of Armageddon. Will those who have made and injected and suffered the injection of calf and horse serums into the human blood stream go scot free? We doubt it.

Quite likely there is some connection between the violation of human blood and the spread of demonism. We cannot suppose that the Creator had no reason for associating the two, and He has done so at least twice in His Word. One of these passages is in Leviticus 19:26 and reads: "Ye shall not eat any thing with the blood; neither shall ye use enchantment, nor observe times."

Can it be that the general corruption and violation of human blood by serums of various sorts has provided a garden out of which, in Armageddon, will grow, and do now grow, the most monstrous conditions of accord with the Devil and his angels, with their vibrations, their ways of doing things, if you please, that have ever taken place on this planet? It looks as if it might be so, and as if we were just beginning to find it out.

Let no one hide behind the thought that the laws given to the Jews have no application to anybody now. In the New Testament it is deserving of particular notice that at the very time when the holy spirit declared by the apostles that the Gentiles are free from the yoke of circumcision, abstinence from blood was explicitly enjoined (Acts 15:28, 29), and the action thus prohibited was classed with idolatry and fornication. This plainly suggests that much of the looseness of our day along sexual lines may be traceable to the easy and continued violation of the divine commands to keep human and animal blood apart from each other. With cells of foreign blood racing through his veins man is not normal, not himself, but lacks the poise and balance which make for self-control.

The Sacredness of Human Blood   By Charles A. Pattillo (Va.)
(REASONS WHY VACCINATION IS UNSCRIPTURAL)

SINCE vaccination has become a topic for discussion, I cannot restrain myself from writing you in regard to this great evil. The vaccination law cannot be a just law. Every father and mother ought to have a right to say what should be done to the body of their own child; yet the vaccination law reduces the father and mother to mere slavery, almost as bad as the colored people were in, when their children were put upon the block and sold. In many slave-sale cases the mother and father were even forbidden to shed tears.

Vaccination is a direct violation of the everlasting covenant that God made with Noah after the flood. In Genesis 9:1-17 we read: "And God blessed Noah and his sons, and said unto them, Be fruitful, and multiply, and replenish the earth. And the fear of you, and the dread of you, shall be upon every beast of the earth, and upon every fowl of the air, upon all that moveth upon the earth, and upon all the fishes of the sea; into your hand are they delivered. Every moving thing that liveth shall be meat for you; even as the green herb have I given you all things. But flesh with the life thereof, which is the blood thereof, shall ye not eat. And surely your blood of your lives will I require; at the hand of every beast will I require it, and at the hand of man; at the hand of every man's brother will I require the life of man. Whoso sheddeth man's blood, by man shall his blood be shed: for in the image of God made he man. And you, be ye fruitful, and multiply; bring forth abundantly in the earth, and multiply therein. And God spake unto Noah, and to his sons with him, saying, And I, behold, I establish my covenant with you, and with your seed after you: and with every living creature that is with you, of the fowl, of the cattle, and of every beast of the earth with you, from all that go out of the ark, to every beast of the earth. And I will establish my covenant with you; neither shall all flesh be cut off any more by the waters of a flood, neither shall there any more be a flood to destroy the earth. And God said, This is the token of the covenant which I

Questions from Readers

● Is there any Scriptural objection to donating one's body for use in medical research or to accepting organs for transplant from such a source?—W. L., U.S.A.

A number of issues are involved in this matter, including the propriety of organ transplants and autopsies. Quite often human emotion is the only factor considered when individuals decide these matters. It would be good, though, for Christians to consider the Scriptural principles that apply, and then make decisions in harmony with these principles so as to be pleasing to Jehovah.—Acts 24:16.

First, it would be well to have in mind that organ transplant operations, such as are now being performed in an attempt to repair the body or extend a life-span, were not the custom thousands of years ago, so we cannot expect to find legislation in the Bible on transplanting human organs. Yet, this does not mean that we have no indication of God's view of such matters.

When Jehovah for the first time allowed humans to eat animal flesh, he explained matters this way to Noah: "A fear of you and a terror of you will continue upon every living creature of the earth and upon every flying creature of the heavens, upon everything that goes moving on the ground, and upon all the fishes of the sea. Into your hand they are now given. Every moving *animal* that is alive may serve as food for you. As in the case of green vegetation, I do give it all to you. Only flesh with its soul—its blood—you must not eat." (Gen. 9:2-4) That allowance was made to Noah, from whom every person now alive descended. Hence, it applies to all of us.

Humans were allowed by God to eat animal flesh and to sustain their human lives by taking the lives of animals, though they were not permitted to eat blood. Did this include eating human flesh, sustaining one's life by means of the body or part of the body of another human, alive or dead? No! That would be cannibalism, a practice abhorrent to all civilized people.

Jehovah clearly made a distinction between the lives of animals and the lives of humans, mankind being created in God's image, with his qualities. (Gen. 1:27) This distinction is evident in His next words. God proceeded to show that man's life is sacred and is not to be taken at will, as may be done with the animals to be used for food. To show disrespect for the sanctity of human life would make one liable to have his own life taken.—Gen. 9:5, 6.

When there is a diseased or defective organ, the usual way health is restored is by taking in nutrients. The body uses the food eaten to repair or heal the organ, gradually replacing the cells. When men of science conclude that this normal process will no longer work and they suggest removing the organ and replacing it directly with an organ from another human, this is simply a shortcut. Those who submit to such operations are thus living off the flesh of another human. That is cannibalistic. However, in allowing man to eat animal flesh Jehovah God did not grant permission for humans to try to perpetuate their lives by cannibalistically taking into their bodies human flesh, whether chewed or in the form of whole organs or body parts taken from others.

It is of interest to note that in its discussion of cannibalism the *Encyclopædia of Religion and Ethics,* edited by James Hastings, Volume 3, page 199, has a section designated "Medical cannibalism." It points out that this is associated with the idea of obtaining strength or some medical virtue from the flesh of another human, adding: "The most remarkable example of this practice occurs in China. Among the poor it is not uncommon for a member of the family to cut a piece of flesh from arm or leg, which is cooked and then given to a sick relative.... The whole superstition in China is certainly connected with the idea that the eating of the human body strengthens the eater.... Among savages the practice is found of giving a sick man some blood to drink drawn from the veins of a relative." Some might argue that therapeutic practices involved in modern organ transplant operations are more scientific than such primitive treatment. Nonetheless, it is evident that men practicing medicine have not been beyond using treatments that amount to cannibalism if such have been thought justified.

Modern science has developed many different types of operations that involve human body parts, some common and usually successful and others experimental and often unsuccessful.

The Watchtower, 11/15/67, p. 702

atomic power. Thus Dr. Forssmann envisions criminals sentenced to death being kept alive until their organs are needed for transplant; then they would be executed by heart-transplant surgeons. Concentration camps would be filled with undesirables who live only until their hearts or kidneys are needed for transplant operations. He is deeply concerned lest "the doctor would finally be degraded to a hangman, a Lucifer, a fallen angel." According to Dr. Mitscherlich, that is the very use doctors were put to during the Nazi regime. They were employed to get rid of undesirables by injections of various things, such as gasoline or tubercule bacilli; in particular, were physicians on submarines used to get rid of troublemakers in this way.

The Legal Aspects

It is interesting to examine the question of the legal aspects of heart transplants. Doctors are concerned that there be new legislation to protect them from possible lawsuits because of performing heart transplants. In some lands it is unlawful to operate on any person except for that person's well-being. This would bar even kidney donors, as the taking of a kidney from a donor is not operating on him for his own benefit, but for that of another person.[12]

Then, again, conceivably one relative may have given consent but others may not have, and these might file a claim against the surgeon. In many states of the United States the wife as the closest of kin would have to give permission.[13] Thus because the Ochsner Clinic and Ochsner Foundation Hospital had performed an autopsy on a body contrary to the expressed wishes of the deceased and without permission of the widow, the Louisiana Circuit Court of Appeals awarded the widow $1,500 damages.[14]

While doctors are concerned about protecting themselves against such lawsuits, their patients are concerned lest they be murdered. Murder is the deliberate taking of the life of another; the fact that death is imminent is beside the point. The law does not distinguish between five minutes, five hours or five years yet to live. As one surgeon expressed it: "For the person who takes a vital organ too soon, society has a word—and that word is murder."[15]

Making a strong case for heart transplants as being murder is attorney H. M. Porter. Writing in the legal newspaper, the Los Angeles *Daily Journal*, February 2, 1968, he tells of being assured by a leading cardiologist that no surgeon would undertake the operation unless the person whose heart was to be used was still alive at the beginning of the operation. The heart must come from a living donor. The donor must be killed to take the heart; the taking of the heart must kill him.

Since it is deliberate killing, he argues, it must be termed murder. Murder can be defended on the basis of self-defense, but in the case of the heart transplant, not the donor, but the surgeon is the aggressor. Then, again, the defense for the murder might be consent, but the law does not recognize the right of consent in the case of murder, as in suicide pacts.

The Scriptural Aspect

Not to be overlooked are the religious, the Scriptural issues involved. There are those, such as the Christian witnesses of Jehovah, who consider *all* transplants between humans as cannibalism; and is not the utilizing of the flesh of another human for one's own life cannibalistic? Nor are they by any means alone in this view. Thus *Newsweek*, December 18, 1968, stated: "An artificial heart that could be mass produced would alleviate the shortage of

● Should congregation action be taken if a baptized Christian accepts a human organ transplant, such as of a cornea or a kidney?

Regarding the transplantation of human tissue or bone from one human to another, this is a matter for conscientious decision by each one of Jehovah's Witnesses. Some Christians might feel that taking into their bodies any tissue or body part from another human is cannibalistic. They might hold that the transplanted human material is intended to become part of the recipient's body to keep him alive and functioning. They might not see it as fundamentally different from consuming flesh through the mouth. Such feelings may arise from considering that God did not make specific provision for man to eat the flesh of his fellow-man when he made provision for humans to eat the flesh of animals that had been drained of their life-sustaining blood. They may give consideration also to the way people in Bible times viewed sustaining themselves by taking in human flesh. For example, see the account at 2 Kings 6:24-30; Deuteronomy 28:53-57; Lamentations 2:20 and 4:10. At John 6:48-66, Jesus spoke figuratively of eating his flesh and drinking his blood. On hearing this discussion and not perceiving the spiritual significance of his words, some of his Jewish disciples were shocked and turned from following him. These accounts illustrate how some humans felt about eating human flesh.

Other sincere Christians today may feel that the Bible does not definitely rule out medical transplants of human organs. They may reason that in some cases the human material is not expected to become a permanent part of the recipient's body. Body cells are said to be replaced about every seven years, and this would be true of any human body parts that would be transplanted. It may be argued, too, that organ transplants are different from cannibalism since the "donor" is not killed to supply

food. In some cases persons nearing death actually have willed body parts to be used for transplants. Of course, if a transplant should require taking in another person's blood, undeniably that would be contrary to God's command.—Acts 15:19, 20.

Clearly, personal views and conscientious feelings vary on this issue of transplantation. It is well known that the use of human materials for human consumption varies all the way from minor items, such as hormones and corneas, to major organs, such as kidneys and hearts. While the Bible specifically forbids consuming blood, ⌐there is no Biblical command pointedly forbidding the taking in of other human tissue.⌐ For this reason, each individual faced with making a decision on this matter should carefully and prayerfully weigh matters and then decide conscientiously what he or she could or could not do before God. ⌐It is a matter for personal decision. (Gal. 6:5) The congregation judicial committee would not take disciplinary action if someone accepted an organ transplant.⌐

—————————•◄—————————

"WATCHTOWER" STUDIES FOR THE WEEKS

April 20. Choosing the Best Way of Life. Page 16. Songs to Be Used: 60, 112.

April 27: Living Up to Our Choice. Page 21. Songs to Be Used: 55, 8.

The Watchtower, 3/15/80, p. 31

10

Strange Ideas Taught in God's Name

It is important to bear in mind in any discussion with Jehovah's Witnesses that they are trained to accept whatever the Watchtower Society says, without questioning the material or critically examining it. This point is subtly conveyed time and again at Kingdom Hall meetings, but occasionally the Society actually puts it into print, as in these quotes from the February 15, 1981, *Watchtower*, pages 18 and 19:

> How shall we view the spiritual food provided by this "faithful and discreet slave"? Should it be viewed critically—'Oh, well, it might be true but then again it might not be and so we have to scrutinize it very critically'? . . . We should have confidence in the channel God is using. At the Brooklyn headquarters from which the Bible publications of Jehovah's Witnesses emanate there are more mature Christian elders, both of the "remnant" and of the "other sheep," than anywhere else upon earth. . . . We all need help to understand the Bible, and we cannot find the Scriptural guidance we need outside the "faithful and discreet slave" organization [*see* pp. 117–118]).

It is very difficult, therefore, for a Jehovah's Witness to see errors in Watchtower Society publications, even when you point them out. The JW has been conditioned to close his eyes to the possibility of critically examining anything that comes from Brooklyn. To break this hypnotic conditioning it may be necessary to find some shocking examples—cases where the Society taught outright nonsense—pure and simple—that no argument can justify.

One such teaching that ought to have shock value for Jehovah's Witnesses today relates to the matter of God's whereabouts. Ask any JW where God lives, and you will most likely receive the answer "In heaven!" How startling it is, then, for a Witness to discover that the official teaching throughout most of the organization's history was that God resides on the star Alcyone in the Pleiades star system! The Society first taught this in 1891, reinforced it later at various times, and let it stand as "the truth" until it was finally contradicted in 1953. Here are quotes to that effect from two Watchtower books published nearly forty years apart, the first in 1891, and the second in 1928:

'. . . *Alcyone, the central one of the renowned Pleiadic stars . . .* Alcyone, then, as far as science has been able to perceive, would seem to be 'the midnight throne' in which the whole system of gravitation has its seat, and *from which the Almighty governs his universe . . .* '(*Studies in the Scriptures*, Vol. III, 1891, pp. 327, italics added [*see* p. 119]).

The constellation of the seven stars forming the Pleides . . . It has been suggested, and with much weight, that *one of the stars of that group is the dwelling-place of Jehovah . . .* The constellation of the Pleiades is a small one compared with others . . . But the greatness in size of other stars or planets is small when compared with the Pleiades in importance, because *the Pleiades is the place of the eternal throne of God. . .* (*Reconciliation*, 1928, p. 14, italics added [*see* p. 120]).

Although it was accepted as "the truth" for decades, this teaching appears so nonsensical to Witnesses today that reading it can help awaken in them the desire to critically examine other Watchtower doctrines.

Another example that could beneficially be shown to a Witness is found in *The Finished Mystery*, the seventh volume of *Studies in the Scriptures*, published in 1917. As is typical of other JW publications, this book interprets much of the Bible as if the inspired Word were written with specific reference to the Watchtower Society. But *The Finished Mystery* carries this to an extreme that even a present day JW would find ridiculous. Thus when Revelation 14:20 symbolically describes blood flowing from a winepress in a deep torrent for a distance of "a thousand and six hundred furlongs" (about 200 miles), the book interprets this as prophesying the precise distance from where *The Finished Mystery* was produced in Scranton, Pennsylvania, to its shipping destination at the organization's Bethel offices in Brooklyn, New York. The verse-by-verse commentary actually cites the "Official Railway Guide" for the distance from the Lackawanna station in Scranton to Hoboken Terminal in New Jersey, and then adds the "New York City Engineer's official distance Hoboken to the Bethel, via Barclay Street Ferry, Fulton Street and Fulton Ferry". . . coming up with a figure that is claimed to be the exact distance predicted in the Bible at Revelation 14:20 (*The Finished Mystery*, 1926 edition, p. 230 [see p. 121]).

Evidently fascinated by railroads, the Watchtower Society also includes in the same book a verse-by-verse discussion of Job 40:15 through 41:34, in which *leviathan* is interpreted to be a prophecy of the steam locomotive. For a full two pages, the commentary presents a "corrected translation" of Job with the claimed prophetic fulfillment inserted in brackets, as in the following excerpt covering 41:1-6 (page 85):

"Thou wilt lengthen out leviathan [the locomotive] with a hook [automatic coupler] or with a snare [coupling-pin] which thou wilt cause his tongue [coupling link] to drop down. Wilt thou not place a ring [piston] in his nostrils [cylinders] or pierce through his cheeks [piston-ends] with a staff [piston rod]? Will he make repeated supplications unto thee [to get off the track]? Or will he utter soft tones unto thee [when he screeches with the whistle]? . . . Wilt thou play with him as with a bird [make him whistle at will]? Or wilt thou bind [enslave] him for thy maidens [so that you can take them to a picnic or convention]? Companies [of stockholders] will feast upon him [his earnings] . . . " [see p. 122]).

Today's sect leaders, in agreement with most other commentators, understand *leviathan* to mean a crocodile. Most Witnesses would be truly shocked to see that the organization once claimed it represented the steam locomotive.

Now, if the Watchtower Society can teach that God lives on

the star Alcyone in the Pleiades star system, that Revelation 14:20 tells the distance from Scranton, Pennsylvania, to Brooklyn Bethel via certain railroads and ferries, and that Job's leviathan prophesied the steam locomotive, what of the Society's other teachings? Might not even the less fanciful ones be just as wrong? That is the question that should rear its head in the minds of Jehovah's Witnesses who are exposed to the information presented here.

You can help your loved one reason on this by asking a few challenging questions. For example: Since the Society claims to be God's "channel of communication," did he tell Watchtower writers that he lived on the star Alcyone? If not, then why did they keep "communicating" that teaching in the magazines and books for so many years? If the Society was wrong in interpreting Job's leviathan as applying to the steam locomotive of the World War I era, might it not also be wrong in applying other Bible verses to that time period? And, what about the organization's presenting Revelation 14:20 as a prophecy about the distance its own book traveled via rail and ferry? Might this not also indicate that the interpretation of other verses as relating to the Society might also be the result of narrow, self-centered thinking? Keep bringing the discussion back to the main point: that the organization is not God's prophesied "faithful and discreet slave," but, rather, a manmade counterfeit.

of the Jerusalem congregation. After that, Paul, Silas and others delivered these decisions to the brothers.—Acts 15:1-35.

What about Paul's missionary travels? Did he act independently of Jehovah's assignment of him as an apostle to a certain group? No, but he obediently accepted his assignment, and this was later recognized by "pillars" of the governing body at Jerusalem, as Galatians 2:9 says: "When they came to know the undeserved kindness that was given me, James and Cephas and John, the ones who seemed to be pillars, gave me and Barnabas the right hand of sharing together, that we should go to the nations, but they to those who are circumcised."—Acts 9:15; 13:1-4; 22:17-21.

Later, when Paul came to Jerusalem for the last time, the Jews there had received misleading reports about him. So the "older men" in Jerusalem advised Paul what to do in an effort to put to rest these reports. And Paul readily accepted their direction.—Acts 21:17-36.

To help us to understand God's Word in these "last days," Jehovah God has lovingly provided a visible organization under Christ—the "faithful and discreet slave." The way Jehovah God has prospered the activities carried on under its direction can leave no doubt in the minds of dedicated Christians as to Jehovah God's approval being upon it.—Matt. 24:45-47.

A NOBLE-MINDED VIEW

How shall we view the spiritual food provided by this "faithful and discreet slave"? Should it be viewed critically— 'Oh, well, it might be true but then again it might not be and so we have to scrutinize it very critically'? Some apparently have felt that way about it. To support their way of thinking they have quoted Acts 17:11, which says of newly interested persons at Beroea: "Now the latter were more noble-minded than those in Thessalonica, for they received the word with the greatest eagerness of mind, carefully examining the Scriptures daily as to whether these things were so."

But does this mean that those Beroeans were looking for flaws in the message they were hearing, or that their attitude was one of doubting? Does this set a precedent for regarding critically the publications brought forth by the "faithful and discreet slave," with a view to finding fault? Not at all!

First of all, let us note the setting of the statement about the noble-minded Beroeans. Paul, accompanied by Silas, was on his second missionary tour. Due to persecution that arose, the brothers at Thessalonica sent them on to Beroea. In Beroea they met sincere Jews who had strong faith in God's Word. These were not Christians yet. They were simply interested persons who had to satisfy themselves that what Paul was telling them had the support of the Hebrew Scriptures.

Up to this time, these devout Jews in Beroea may never have heard of Jesus Christ. What Paul was telling them was *entirely new*. So those noble-minded Jews in Beroea searched the Scriptures daily to make certain that the references that Paul gave were really part of God's Word. And with what mental attitude did they pursue their studies? With a skeptical attitude, trying to prove Paul wrong? No, they were altogether unlike Paul's critics on Mars Hill, for we read that they heard Paul's testimony with "the greatest eagerness of mind."—Acts 17:11, 32.

These Beroeans listened with a readiness, yes, an eagerness, to believe. Thus not only were they open-minded, but they were *wanting* to have this "good news" proved true. In fact, for a person to acquire faith he must have "the will to believe." If he is determined not to believe, then no amount of evidence will convince him; for if a person looks for them he

The Watchtower, 2/15/81, p.18

can always find excuses, plausible reasons for not accepting the accountability that belief will bring upon him. As the apostle Paul well said: "Faith is not a possession of all people." (2 Thess. 3:2) But the Beroeans had the will to believe. They considered what they heard with a receptive frame of mind. As a result, "many of them became believers, and so did not a few of the reputable Greek women and of the men."—Acts 17:12.

Jesus' disciples wrote many letters to Christian congregations, to persons who were already in "the way of the truth." (2 Pet. 2:2) But nowhere do we read that those brothers first, in a skeptical frame of mind, checked the Scriptures to make certain that those letters had Scriptural backing, that the writers really knew what they were talking about.

OUR VIEW OF THE "SLAVE"

We can benefit from this consideration. If we have once established what instrument God is using as his "slave" to dispense spiritual food to his people, surely Jehovah is not pleased if we receive that food as though it might contain something harmful. We should have confidence in the channel God is using. At the Brooklyn headquarters from which the Bible publications of Jehovah's Witnesses emanate there are more mature Christian elders, both of the "remnant" and of the "other sheep," than anywhere else upon earth.

True, the brothers preparing these publications are not infallible. Their writings are not inspired as are those of Paul and the other Bible writers. (2 Tim. 3:16) And so, at times, it has been necessary, as understanding became clearer, to correct views. (Prov. 4:18) However, this has resulted in a continual refining of the body of Bible-based truth to which Jehovah's Witnesses subscribe. Over the years, as adjustments have been made to that body of truth, it has become ever more wonderful and applicable to our lives in these "last days." Bible commentators of Christendom are not inspired either. Despite their claims to great knowledge, they have failed to highlight even basic Bible truths —such as the coming Paradise earth, the importance of God's name, and the condition of the dead.

Rather, the record that the "faithful and discreet slave" organization has made for the past more than 100 years forces us to the conclusion that Peter expressed when Jesus asked if his apostles also wanted to leave him, namely, "Whom shall we go away to?" (John 6:66-69) No question about it. We all need help to understand the Bible, and we cannot find the Scriptural guidance we need outside the "faithful and discreet slave" organization.

THE SCYTHIAN

WHEN stressing that fleshly distinctions do not affect a Christian's standing as a member of Christ's body, the apostle Paul wrote: "There is neither Greek nor Jew, circumcision nor uncircumcision, foreigner, Scythian, slave, freeman, but Christ is all things and in all." (Col. 3:11) The inclusion of the Scythians is noteworthy, as these fierce, nomadic people were regarded as the worst of barbarians. However, through the power exerted by God's holy spirit, even they could put on a Christlike personality, discarding their former ways. (Col. 3:9, 10) How powerful is the spirit of God!

The Watchtower, 2/15/81, p. 19

The Great Pyramid.   327

this distance to be from ninety to ninety–six millions of miles, their latest calculation and conclusion being ninety-two millions.   The Great Pyramid has also its own way of indicating the most correct standard of all weights and measures, based upon the size and weight of the earth, which it is also claimed to indicate.

Commenting upon the scientific testimony and the location of this majestic "Witness," Rev. Joseph Seiss, D. D. suggests:

"There is a yet grander thought embodied in this wonderful structure.   Of its five points there is one of special pre–eminence, in which all its sides and exterior lines terminate.   It is the summit corner, which lifts its solemn index finger to the sun at midday, and by its distance from the base tells the mean distance to that sun from the earth. And if we go back to the date which the Pyramid gives itself, and look for what that finger pointed to at midnight, we find a far sublimer indication.   Science has at last discovered that the sun is not a dead center, with planets wheeling about it, but itself stationary.   It is now ascertained that the sun also is in motion, carrying with it its splendid retinue of comets, planets, its satellites and theirs, around some other and vastly mightier center.   Astronomers are not yet fully agreed as to what or where that center is.   Some, however, believe that they have found the direction of it to be the Pleiades, and particularly Alcyone, the central one of the renowned Pleiadic stars.   To the distinguished German astronomer, Prof. J. H. Maedler, belongs the honor of having made this discovery.   Alcyone, then, as far as science has been able to perceive, would seem to be ' the midnight throne' in which the whole system of gravitation has its central seat, and from which the Almighty governs his universe.   And here is the wonderful corresponding fact, that at the date of the Great Pyramid's building, at midnight of the autumnal equinox, and hence the true beginning of the year * as still preserved in the traditions of many nations, the Pleiades were distributed

_____

* The beginning of the Jewish year, introduced by the Day of Atonement, as shown in MILLENNIAL DAWN, VOL. II.

14   *Reconciliation*

man sees that the earth occupies a place of great importance in God's plan and purposes and that in his
due time every creature in heaven and in earth will
be brought into one grand harmonious whole or unity.
To this effect the inspired witness of Jehovah wrote:
"Having made known unto us the mystery of his will,
according to his good pleasure which he hath pur-
posed in himself: that in the dispensation of the fulness of times he might gather together in one all things
in Christ, both which are in heaven, and which are
on earth; even in him."—Eph. 1: 9, 10.

˹The constellation of the seven stars forming the
Pleiades˺ appears to be the crowning center around
which the known systems of the planets revolve even
as our sun's planets obey the sun and travel in their
respective orbits. ˹It has been suggested, and with
much weight, that one of the stars of that group is
the dwelling-place of Jehovah˺ and the place of the
highest heavens; that it is the place to which the inspired writer referred when he said: "Hear thou
from thy dwellingplace, even from heaven" (2 Chron.
6: 21); and that it is the place to which Job referred
when under inspiration he wrote: "Canst thou bind
the sweet influences of Pleiades, or loose the bands of
Orion?"—Job 38: 31.

˹The constellation of the Pleiades is a small one compared with others˺ which scientific instruments disclose to the wondering eyes of man. ˹But the greatness
in size of other stars or planets is small when compared with the Pleiades in importance, because the
Pleiades is the place of the eternal throne of God.˺
For a like reason the various groups of stars, greater
in size than the planet earth, must in the eyes of

230   *The Finished Mystery*   **REV. 14**

cometh; when your fear cometh as desolation, and your destruction cometh as a whirlwind; when distress and anguish cometh upon you. ˙ Then shall they call upon Me, but I will not answer; they shall seek Me early, but they shall not find Me; for that they hated knowledge, and did not choose the fear of the Lord. They would none of my counsel: they despised all my reproof. Therefore shall they eat of the fruit of their own way."—Prov. 1:24-31.

By the space of a thousand and [six] TWO hundred furlongs.—This can not be interpreted to refer to the 2100 mile battle line of the world war. A furlong or stadium is not a mile and this is without the city whereas the battle line is within the city. See Rotherham's translation.

A stadium is 606¾ English ft.; 1200 stadii are, mi., 137.9

The work on this volume was done in Scranton, Pa. As fast as it was completed it was sent to the Bethel. Half of the work was done at an average distance of 5 blocks from the Lackawanna station, and the other half at a distance of 25 blocks. Blocks in Scranton are 10 to the mile. Hence the average distance to the station is 15 blocks, or........... **1.5 mi.**

Official Railway Guide time table distance Scranton to Hoboken Terminal, 133.0 "

New York City Engineer's official distance Hoboken to the Bethel, via Barclay Street Ferry, Fulton Street and Fulton Ferry, 8,850, 4,950, 2,540 and 1,460 feet respectively, or a total of............. **3.4 "**

Shortest distance from place where the winepress was trodden by the Feet Members of the Lord, Whose guidance and help alone made this volume possible. (John 6:60, 61; Matt. 20:11.).......... **mi., 137.9**

The treading, be it remembered, is a mental process. As rapidly as the erroneous doctrines and practices which have been the life-blood of Christendom are recognized in their relationship to the true kingdom of Christ, and as rapidly as those ideas are discarded by the individual, just so rapidly is the blood trodden out of Christendom's false systems. This book is the result of such laborious treading, and is a means to enable others, in their turn, to do some treading.

The Finished Mystery, 1926 edition, p. 230

The Author of the Plan   **85**

⌜"Thou wilt lengthen out leviathan [the locomotive] with a hook [automatic coupler] or with a snare [coupling-pin] which thou wilt cause his tongue [coupling-link] to drop down. Wilt thou not place a ring [piston] in his nostrils [cylinders] or pierce through his cheeks [piston-ends] with a staff [piston-rod]? Will he make repeated supplication unto thee [to get off the track]? Or will he utter soft tones unto thee [when he screeches with the whistle]?⌝ Will he make a covenant with thee, that thou mayest take him for a servant forever [without repairs]? ⌜Wilt thou play with him as with a bird [make him whistle at will]? Or wilt thou bind [enslave] him for thy maidens [so that you can take them to a picnic or convention]? Companies [of stockholders] will feast upon him [his earnings];⌝they will share him among speculators. [Psa. 74:14.] Thou wilt fill his skin with pointed irons [bolts], and his head with a cabin of fishermen [a cab similar to the cabins on fishing vessels]. Place thy hand upon him, be mindful of the conflict [raging within the boiler] and thou wilt add no further questions. Behold, his confidence [boiler] being deceived [not properly supplied with water], shall not at once his mighty form be spread asunder [by an explosion]? There is none so bold that he will stir him up [to run at his very highest possible speed], and none who will then place himself before him [to be run over]. Who will compete with this one and endure [pass him on the track]? Under the whole heaven, none, unless [one like] himself.

"I will not pass in silence his members, nor the cause of his mighty forces, nor the beauty of his equipment. Who can strip off the facings of his jacket? Who can penetrate between the double lap of his shield [the overlapping sections of the boiler plates]? Who can force open the doors of his shield [the boiler ends]? The circuits of his teeth [rows of rivets] are formidable. His strength depends on courses of shields [sections of plates] closed up tightly with a seal [calked]. They shall join one upon another so that a hiss of air [steam] shall not escape from between them. One to the other shall adhere. They will be welded together that they cannot be sundered. In his sneezing [when he puffs from the cylinders] light will shine, a flood of light prevading the mass of vapors: and his eyes [headlights] will be as the eyelashes of the morning [as rays of light from the rising sun]. Out of his mouth [fire-door] will leap forth flaming torches, and [from the smoke stack] glowing sparks will slip themselves away. From his nostrils [cylinders] will issue forth vapor as from a boiling pot or caldron. His inhaling

The Finished Mystery, 1926 edition, p. 85

11

"God's Visible Organization"

ATTORNEY: "Who subsequently became the Editor of the magazine, the main editor of the 'Watch Tower' magazine?"

FRED W. FRANZ: "In 1931, October 15th, as I recall, the 'Watch Tower' discontinued publishing the names of any editorial committee on the second page."

THE COURT: "He asked you who became the editor."

FRED W. FRANZ: "And it said —"

THE COURT: "Who became the editor?"

ATTORNEY: "Who became the editor when this was discontinued?"

FRED W. FRANZ: "Jehovah God."

That exchange took place under oath in a New York court of law in 1940. Fred W. Franz, who became president of the Watchtower Society in 1977, was then one of several leaders sued by a former prominent member [see pp. 126–127]. In answer to the examining attorney, Franz asserted that the *Watchtower* magazine has God as its editor. This gives some idea as to what Jehovah's Witnesses mean when they refer to "God's organization."

Likewise, note these words of the Society's second president, J. F. Rutherford, published in 1917:

The Watch Tower Bible and Tract Society is the greatest corporation in the world, because from the time of its organization until now the Lord has used it as his channel through which to make known the glad tidings. . . (*The Watch Tower*, 1/15/17, p. 22 [see p. 128]).

To graphically illustrate this point, *The Watchtower* of December 15, 1971, actually featured on page 749 an organizational chart much like those used to outline the corporate structure of secular businesses. Only here "Jehovah" occupies the topmost box, corresponding to chairman of the board; in the next box below is "Jesus Christ," as chief executive officer, followed by the Governing Body in Brooklyn, New York, and then the various overseers of the JW hierarchy. [see p. 130.]

Seen in this way, the organization becomes an extension of God himself, and disregard of organizational instructions becomes tantamount to sin.

According to *The Watchtower* of November 15, 1981, page 21, the message preached by JWs "includes the invitation to come to Jehovah's organization for salvation." [see p. 131]. The organization is thus, in effect, the "savior" of the Witnesses.

As to the Watchtower Society's importance relative to the Bible, the sect has also published the following:

. . . Thus the Bible is an organizational book and belongs to the Christian congregation as an organization, not to individuals, regardless of how sincerely they may believe that they can interpret the Bible. For this reason the Bible cannot be properly understood without Jehovah's visible organization in mind (*The Watchtower*, 10/1/67, p. 587 [see p. 132]).

The above statements are important to review with your Jehovah's Witness loved one, to prevent his or her dismissing the evidence presented in our preceding chapters by saying that the organization is simply a group of imperfect men. Yes, imperfect men are capable of false prophecies, doctrinal changes, odd teachings, and so on. But, as we have seen above, the Watchtower organization has made claims for itself that elevate it above mere men.

These claims put the information furnished in the other chapters in proper perspective. As the old saying goes, "The bigger they are, the harder they fall." Or, as the Bible puts it, "Pride goeth before destruction, and an haughty spirit before a fall" (Prov. 16:18 KJV); "And whosoever shall exalt himself shall be abased . . ." (Matt. 23:12 KJV).

Having exalted itself to the station of God's prophet, God's exclusive channel of communication, the only authority on earth capable of interpreting the Bible, and God's visible organization, the Watchtower Society can not simply shrug off as "mistakes" the false prophecies, back-and-forth doctrinal changes, and outright nonsense it has published over the years.

Kings County Clerk's Index No. 15845—Year 1940

New York Supreme Court

Appellate Division—Second Department

OLIN R. MOYLE

Plaintiff-Respondent

against

FRED W. FRANZ, NATHAN H. KNORR, GRANT SUITER, THOMAS J. SULLIVAN, WILLIAM P. HEATH, JR., HUGO H. RIEMER, WILLIAM E. VAN AMBURGH, ARTHUR R. GOUX, CHARLES A. WISE, CLAYTON J. WOODWORTH, MATTHEW A. HOWLETT, WATCH TOWER BIBLE & TRACT SOCIETY, a Pennsylvania corporation, and WATCHTOWER BIBLE AND TRACT SOCIETY, INC., a New York membership corporation

Defendants-Appellants

CASE ON APPEAL

Vol. II—Pages 607 to 1328

HAYDEN C. COVINGTON
Attorney for Defendants-Appellants
117 Adams Street
Borough of Brooklyn
New York City

WALTER BRUCHHAUSEN
Attorney for Plaintiff-Respondent
14 Wall Street
Borough of Manhattan
New York City

APPEAL PRINTING CO., INC., 180 CEDAR ST., NEW YORK, WO 2-5040

N.Y. King's County Clerk's court record, 1940, Vol. II, title page

795

Fred W. Franz—For Defts.—Direct

such editorial committee? A. No, that was the Will of Pastor Russell.

Q. Who subsequently became the Editor of the magazine, the main editor of the "Watch Tower" magazine? A. In 1931, October 15th, as I recall, the "Watch Tower" discontinued publishing the names of any editorial committee on the second page.

> The Court: He asked you who became the editor.
> The Witness: And it said—
> The Court: Who became the editor?

Q. Who became the editor when this was discontinued? A. Jehovah God.

Q. And who wrote the magazine under the direction of Almighty God? A. Various individuals contributed to the magazine, Judge Rutherford, and others.

Q. Who passed on what went into it? A. Judge Rutherford, primarily, and he also called in associates—

> The Court: Who had the final say?
> The Witness: Judge Rutherford supervised everything that went into the magazine, sir.

Q. Is the "Watch Tower" magazine dogmatic?

> Mr. Bruchhausen: I object to that.
> The Court: Objection sustained.
> Mr. Covington: That is a statement that has been read to the jury from the magazine and I want to explain that.

one thing, sometimes another. But no matter. It is ours to show forth the praises of God. And some few will hear, and will take knowledge that we have been with Jesus and learned of him. Thus they may be led to God.

While this holy Spirit proceeds from the Word of God and from the lives of God's children, it does not come to them without divine assistance in the matter. For instance, while studying the Word of God, we may be in touch with the spiritual channel of heavenly communion—namely, prayer; by which the child of God may tell the Father of his feelings, sentiments, etc., even as God through the Bible tells his children his sentiments. Thus we receive an increase of the holy Spirit through the act of prayer. In our appeals for forgiveness, etc., we are reviving in our minds the Spirit of God; and this, holy Spirit comes to us more richly as a further comfort and assistance in the good way. We call to mind the divine assurance, "Like as a father pitieth his children, so the Lord pitieth them that reverence him"; and so we come to the throne of heavenly grace to obtain mercy and find grace to help in every time of need. As therefore the needy one comes, he receives more of the holy Spirit.

There is still another means by which the heavenly Father gives his children of his holy Spirit, and that is through his providences. While we know not, of ourselves, the things we should ask for as we ought, we know from his Word that we may always ask for more of his holy Spirit and the fruits and graces thereof. But we may not at first realize how these can best be cultivated in our hearts. We have the instruction in the Bible that we are to put on meekness, self-control, gentleness, patience, long-suffering, brotherly kindness. Yet while we know this, there is something more that we need

—experiences in life which will bring these things before our minds so that they may be better appreciated by us and we may get more of the holy Spirit out of these injunctions of Holy Writ. For instance, we shall have special trials, and thus learn what real patience is, and why we should exercise patience. And so with meekness. The Lord may permit us to stumble into some trial by which we may be led to see our lack in this respect; and we may come to study more carefully the quality of meekness, to see the holy Spirit of meekness as presented in the Bible. And thus with self-control, gentleness and love.

So God is giving us more of his holy Spirit by bringing the instructions of the Bible forcefully to our attention through painful experiences. These experiences are supervised by the Lord, by his holy Spirit, or power, as a part of the means by which we are to attain the necessary heart and character development—that thus we may be rounded out and become rich in all the heavenly fruits and graces.

"O holy Spirit, Messenger of God,
  Come, fill our hearts and minds with rich intent!
Illuminate, instruct, and guide our wills,
  That they may with thy mind be fully blent.

"By words divine that point the heavenly way,
  By discipline's hard hammer, or by strain
Of heavenly music winged with pleading prayer,
  By sunshine bright or dreary days of pain,

"Lead thou us on! This narrow, rugged path
  We cannot keep alone; but led by thee,
The way grows luminous and sweet and fair,
  Each earthly bond is loosed, and we are free!"

CONVENTION AT PITTSBURGH

ELECTION OF OFFICERS

The Convention of Bible Students at Pittsburgh, January 6 and 7, was a season of blessed fellowship. When the Society began to make arrangements for the annual election of its officers, required by the charter to be held at Pittsburgh, on January 6, it was thought well to have a convention in connection therewith, and a two-days' convention was then arranged.

would place his name in nomination. This was seconded by various brethren from Pittsburgh, Boston, Cleveland, Washington, Pa., New York, and other cities. There being no further nominations, a motion was made that the rule of balloting be suspended, and that the Secretary of the convention be directed to cast the entire vote for Brother J. F. Rutherford. Thereupon the Secretary cast the ballot as directed, and Brother Rutherford was declared the unanimous choice of the

This was the first convention held by the Society since the death of Brother Russell. As was expected, the spirit manifested by the friends in attendance was excellent, giving evidence that all had been living very near to the Lord. The attendance on Saturday, the 6th, averaged about 600, and sessions were held in Carnegie Hall, North Side, Pittsburgh. The addresses by Brother Ritchie and Brother Hirsh were much enjoyed by the friends.

The Sunday meetings were held at the Lyceum Theater, opening at 9:45 a. m., with the Bethel service and followed by a praise and testimony meeting. At 11 o'clock there was an address by Brother Macmillan, Chairman of the convention; about a thousand of the friends were in attendance at this time. In the afternoon Brother Rutherford delivered an address to about 1,500, about 500 of the public being present. Excellent attention was given, and a good proportion of cards received from those who had heard the truth for the first time.

The evening address by Brother Van Amburgh was greatly appreciated and was followed by a love feast, participated in by about 500.

THE SOCIETY'S OFFICERS

Saturday was the day specially set apart for the election of officers to serve the WATCH TOWER BIBLE AND TRACT SOCIETY for the ensuing year. Much interest was centered in this election by friends throughout the world. Brother Russell had held the office of President from the organization of the Society, in 1884, to the time of his death. Approximately 150,000 votes were represented in person and by proxy. The session was opened by Vice-President Brother A. I. Ritchie with devotional services. He stated that the first work would be the appointment of a Committee on rules and regulations. As it would take a little time for the Committee to complete its work, four o'clock in the afternoon was set to hear its report. It was nearly five when the Chairman called the meeting to order. The report of the Committee was read and adopted by the convention.

The next order of business was the nomination and election of a President. Brother Pierson, with very appropriate remarks and expressions of appreciation and love for Brother Russell, stated that he had received word as proxy-holder from friends all over the land to the effect that he cast their votes for Brother J. F. Rutherford for President, and he further stated that he was in full sympathy with this and therefore convention as President of the Society for the ensuing year. Nominations for Vice-President were then called for, and Brother A. N. Pierson and Brother A. I. Ritchie were nominated, both nominations being seconded by various brethren. The counting of the ballots showed that Brother Pierson received the larger number of votes. A motion then made the election of Brother Pierson as Vice-President of the Society unanimous.

There was but one nomination for Secretary-Treasurer, and the Chairman was requested to cast the vote of the convention for Brother W. E. Van Amburgh, who was declared elected.

The friends everywhere had prayed earnestly for the Lord's guidance and direction in the matter of the election; and when it was concluded, everyone was content and happy, believing that the Lord had directed their deliberations and answered their prayers. Perfect harmony prevailed amongst all present.

A resolution was passed to the effect that while the President is the Executive Officer and General Manager of the Society's work and affairs, both in America and all foreign countries where the Society has branches, he might appoint an Advisory Committee from time to time to advise and consult with him concerning the conduct of the affairs of the Society. It was understood that this resolution was passed at the suggestion of Brother Rutherford, to the end that the President might have certain ones upon whom he might call at any time for aid and advice in the weightier matters pertaining to the affairs of the Watch Tower Bible and Tract Society.

Following the election Brother Rutherford, addressing the meeting, said in part:

"Dear friends, I cannot let this occasion pass without saying a few words to you. My heart is full to overflowing. You will bear me witness that I have not in any way sought the office of President of this Society. Up to this hour I have not discussed it with any one. I have purposely avoided doing so, believing that the Lord would accomplish his purpose. What has been done here today I feel that the Lord has directed, and I humbly bow to his will. To him alone is due all honor and glory.

"The WATCH TOWER BIBLE AND TRACT SOCIETY is the greatest corporation in the world, because from the time of its organization until now the Lord has used it as his channel through which to make known the glad tidings to many thousands, which glad tidings the whole world ernment at Jerusalem or by the Senate of the Roman Empire, with officers to be appointed according to Caesar's specifications. No, but it was a theocratic organization with officers and assistants that were theocratically appointed by the governing body and Jesus Christ, the "head of the congregation." The "gifts in men" that had been given to it were, not from the Roman Emperor Caesar, but from the great Theocrat, Jehovah God, through Jesus Christ. For what purpose? "With a view to the readjustment of the holy ones, for ministerial work." (Eph. 4:11, 12) The whole congregation was a service body, all members rendering sacred service to the great Theocrat Jehovah. They were one composite "servant" of their Divine

Ruler, whose witnesses they were. They were bearing witness that He had sent the promised Messiah in the person of Jesus Christ his Son. To them as spiritual Israelites the words applied:

⁵ " 'You are my witnesses,' is the utterance of Jehovah, 'even my servant whom I have chosen.' "—Isa. 43:10.

⁶ Thus the many witnesses form one "servant," whom Jehovah calls "my servant whom I have chosen." This composite "servant" is the one whom Jesus Christ had in mind when he spoke of his going away and his returning, saying: "Who really is the faithful steward, the discreet one, whom his master will appoint

6. Who, then, is that "steward" and "slave" mentioned by Jesus in Luke 12:42-44?

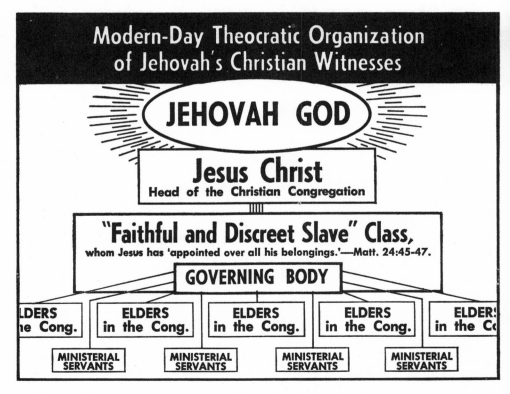

The Watchtower, 12/15/71, p. 749

his provision for salvation through Jesus Christ by meeting together this past April to observe the Memorial of Christ's death.

¹⁶ As Jehovah's forward-moving organization approaches the final years of its preaching activity toward this world, there is no doubt that the scope of the work will grow. Recall what the Israelites were instructed to do just before God destroyed Jericho. First, they were instructed to march around the city once a day for six days. But then they were told: "On the seventh day you should march round the city seven times and the priests should blow the horns. And it must occur that when they sound with the horn of the ram, when you hear the sound of the horn, all the people should shout a great war cry; and the wall of the city must fall down flat."—Josh. 6:2-5.

¹⁷ On that seventh and last day, the Israelites were to increase their activity seven times! Then they were to "shout a great war cry." Exactly as instructed, they did this. "It came about on the seventh day that they proceeded to get up early, as soon as the dawn ascended, and they went marching round the city in this manner seven times. . . . And it came about on the seventh time that the priests blew the horns, and Joshua proceeded to say to the people: 'Shout; for Jehovah has given you the city.' . . . And it came about that as soon as the people heard the sound of the horn and the people began to shout a great war cry, then the

wall began to fall down flat."—Josh. 6:15, 16, 20.

¹⁸ We can expect a similar expansion of our preaching activity now, at this climax of the ages. No doubt, before the "great tribulation" is finished, we will see the greatest witness to God's name and kingdom in the history of this world. And while now the witness yet ʼincludes the invitation to come to Jehovah's organization for salvation⌐ the time no doubt will come when the message takes on a harder tone, like a "great war cry." Revelation 16:21 shows that "a great hail with every stone about the weight of a talent [nearly 100 pounds] descended out of heaven upon the men, and the men blasphemed God due to the plague of hail, because the plague of it was unusually great." Hailstones are frozen, hardened water. So this pictures how, at the end, Jehovah's judgment message sent down upon disobedient mankind will be like a barrage of hard-hitting hail. The fact that the plague of hailstones is spoken of as being "unusually great" suggests that at the very end there will be a hard proclamation of Jehovah's "day of vengeance" by Jehovah's servants.

¹⁹ So, then, we do well to say, as Peter did, "Since all these things are thus to be dissolved, what sort of persons ought you to be in holy acts of conduct and deeds of godly devotion"! (2 Pet. 3:11) Surely, we need to "keep comforting one another and building one another up." We should "always pursue what is good toward one another." (1 Thess. 5:11, 15) "Really, then, as long as we have time favorable for it, let us work what is good toward all, but especially toward those related to us in the faith." (Gal. 6:10) To this end, do not fail to 'stay awake and keep your senses.'—1 Thess. 5:6.

16, 17. (a) What instructions were given to the nation of Israel before God destroyed Jericho? (b) How were those instructions carried out?

18. What do we anticipate as regards the scope and manner of the preaching activity before this system comes to its end?

19. In view of the immediate future, 'what kind of persons ought we to be'?

The Watchtower, 11/15/81, p. 21

children of Israel had been slaves in Egypt. Moses had already freed himself from Egypt's yoke by fleeing to Midian, where he had lived for forty years. But Jehovah directed him to return to Egypt to represent the Israelites as one united body of people. Jehovah then made a common provision for them all, and any who expected to benefit from it had to act upon it in the same identical manner. All must conform in the selection of an animal, a male sheep or goat one year old, and sprinkle its blood on the doorposts of their houses. Then, by families, they must roast and eat its flesh and leave Egypt en masse about midnight as an orderly body, obeying common instructions and receiving a common deliverance. (Ex. 12:1-13, 21-39) When Jehovah brought them all to Mount Sinai in the wilderness, he gave them his Law organizing them as a theocratic nation.

[8] All the Law or *Torah* that Jehovah inspired Moses to write was for this theocratic organization of Israel. So were all the other books that now comprise the Hebrew Scriptures, or the "Old Testament" as some persons refer to them. But over fifteen centuries later, Paul, himself an Israelite and an apostle of Jesus Christ, wrote concerning these books that make up three-quarters of our Bible: "For all the things that were written aforetime were written for our instruction, that through our endurance and through the comfort from the Scriptures we might have hope." (Rom. 15:4) By this, Paul meant that the Bible, as an instruction book for the theocratic organization of Israel, had now become a book of instructions for the organization of the Christian congregation.

[9] As the canon of books of God's Word was expanded and the Christian Greek Scriptures were added to complete the Bible, each book was written directly to the Christian congregation or to a member of the Christian congregation in its behalf. ⸢Thus the Bible is an organizational book and belongs to the Christian congregation as an organization, not to individuals, regardless of how sincerely they may believe that they can interpret the Bible. For this reason the Bible cannot be properly understood without Jehovah's visible organization in mind.⸣

THE CHRISTIAN
CONGREGATION AS AN ORGANIZATION

[10] Jesus did not begin the Christian congregation while he was still on earth. He did, however, select twelve apostles at that time, although Judas, who betrayed him, was replaced by another follower after Jesus' ascension to his Father in heaven. These "apostles of the Lamb" began to serve as foundation stones and pillars of the congregation after it was organized. (Rev. 21:14) This came on the day of Pentecost, 33 C.E., when the first Christian congregation was organized at Jerusalem. One hundred and twenty of Jesus' disciples were assembled together with one mind and purpose when Jehovah's spirit was poured out upon them, and the Christian congregation never lost this unity of thought as long as the apostles remained alive.—Acts 1:12-15; 2:1-4.

[11] Though separated in person and groups assembling as Christian congregations, those composing the Christian congregation are still one united body, just as Israel was one typical theocratic nation. Paul said: "One body there is, and

---

8. How did the Hebrew Scriptures become a book of instructions for Christians?
9. How can it be said that the Bible is an organizational book for the Christian congregation?

10. When and how did the Christian congregation have a beginning?
11, 12. (a) What wrong view do some persons take of the Christian congregation? (b) How do Paul and Peter show that the congregation must be one body?

12

Providing an Alternative

Have you ever tried to take a broken or dangerous toy away from a little child? What a struggle it was!—until it finally occurred to you to offer something else more appealing. Then the child happily dropped the object that had been held in a grip of iron only seconds before.

The same principle applies to an adult's dearly held but erroneous religious belief. Asking the person simply to let it go, without providing an alternative, is like asking the child to release the toy and sit there empty-handed. For the one holding onto the treasured possession, it is an invitation to embrace emptiness. It is unthinkable, but when a more attractive substitute arrives on the scene, the former treasure becomes trash and is easily discarded without regrets.

The situation of the cult adherent is of course infinitely more complex than that of the child clinging to a harmful toy. For the child the toy is a momentary center of attention, but for the cultist his religious organization is *everything*. It holds within itself not only his relationship with God and his hope for the future, but also the things he needs for day-to-day survival: a worldview that brings order out of chaos, a circle of friends who accept him as part of their "in" group, and a weekly schedule of activities that fill what might otherwise be empty hours. How can you ask someone to abandon all this without assuring him of a more real relationship with God, a more dependable hope for the future, a more reasonable worldview, a more loving circle of friends, and a more interesting schedule of activities?

People who leave the Watchtower without finding an acceptable alternative typically go into spiritual and emotional shock. This happens when a Jehovah's Witness is suddenly ensnared in a practice forbidden by the organization and is expelled. He or a family member may be injured in an automobile accident, and in a moment of "spiritual weakness," the Witness agrees to a blood transfusion. Or perhaps he impulsively buys a lottery ticket, goes too far physically with his fiancée, or takes up cigarette smoking. The result is often a speedy trial before a judicial committee of elders, followed by expulsion from the organization. In this "disfellowshiped" state the Witness now finds himself shunned by all his JW friends, relatives, and acquaintances. He is no longer welcome in their homes, and they refuse to greet him or even to acknowledge his presence if they pass him on the street.

Tens of thousands are expelled in this manner every year. I have had personal contact with hundreds of them. Such an individual is out of the Watchtower with nowhere to go. Until provided an acceptable alternative, the former Witness may wander for years in a spiritual vacuum, feeling condemned by God and without hope in the world. These Watchtower castaways often have difficulty making other than surface friendships, hesitating to open their wounded heart to further abuse. Still influenced by their Kingdom Hall training, they look down on so-called worldly people as unclean—even though they themselves now fall into that category by JW standards. In this condition they are prime candidates for reinstatement in the Jehovah's Witnesses or recruitment by another cult. Many in fact do return to the Watchtower or fall victim to a different deception.

So not only is it *difficult* to draw someone out of the Watchtower without offering a sound religious alternative, but it is also *dangerous*. Like thrusting a victim of hypothermia into a hot tub or suddenly depriving an addict of his drug, much harm can come to the person abruptly yanked out of a cult.

But providing a sound religious alternative involves much more than simply saying, "Come to church with me! You'll like it better than Kingdom Hall." To understand how comfortable a Jehovah's Witness feels about such an invitation, just imagine yourself being invited by a Hare Krishna devotee to "Shave your head, put on this saffron robe, and come to the temple with me!

You'll like it better than church." To a JW, a church is just as foreign as a Hindu temple. In his mind a church is a demon-infested building surmounted by a pagan emblem (the cross) atop a phallic symbol (the steeple), and filled with immoral people who worship a three-headed false god (the Trinity) and salute an idol made of cloth (the national flag). In order to rid the Witness of such notions, it is necessary to consider how he or she came to accept them in the first place.

Many people are reasoned into the Watchtower. They may have been perfectly content the way they were, but then comes a knock at the door. A Jehovah's Witness starts a "free home Bible study" with them, adeptly replaces the Bible with a Watchtower Society book, and spends an hour or two each week reasoning point by point with them on subjects such as deity, prayer, holidays, military service, the cross, modern fulfillment of biblical prophecy, acceptable and unacceptable forms of medical treatment, and so on. By the time the indoctrination program has been concluded, virtually every aspect of life has been covered, and the convert's thinking has been entirely restructured.

This process *must* be reversed when leaving the organization. Otherwise, as the saying goes, "You can get the boy off the farm, but you can't get the farm out of the boy." Only in this case it becomes, "You can get the boy out of the Watchtower, but you can't get the Watchtower out of the boy." The former Witness will retain the automatic thought patterns that had been programmed into his brain. Although not attending Kingdom Hall meetings, he will still think, feel, and act like a Jehovah's Witness.

The best remedy for this is personal contact with former Witnesses who have become Christians. They have already gone through the process of untwisting the twisted reasonings they had been taught, but they still remember how they used to think as a JW, so they are in the best position to help a member or new ex-member. However, at first it may not be possible to put your loved one in touch with ex-Witnesses, perhaps because he or she is not yet ready to deal with apostates, or perhaps due to geographical isolation. In this case you can train yourself to provide the necessary help by familiarizing yourself with the testimonies of former JWs. Also, my book *Jehovah's Witnesses An-*

swered Verse by Verse will enable you to overcome the twisted reasonings and aid your relative or friend to cross the gap from cultic error to traditional Christianity.

On the other hand, some people were never reasoned into the Watchtower, and so reason alone will not be sufficient to get them out. These are individuals who were originally drawn to the organization because it filled an emotional need. That emotional need must now be identified and dealt with in order to help that person leave the Jehovah's Witnesses.

You can be fairly certain that someone became a Witness to satisfy an emotional need, if *any* of the following are true: (1) He or she joined shortly after experiencing a divorce, a betrothal breakup, the death of a close family member, or other similar loss. (2) The person had just moved from another city or town and had not yet made new friends when the Witnesses called. (3) The individual began attending all Kingdom Hall meetings shortly after the Witnesses made their initial call, rather than after a lengthy study course.

Cults tend to attract lonely people. Newcomers are given a warm welcome, fawned over with lots of affection, invited back, and asked to share in other gatherings and activities; one or more members are assigned (without the newcomer's knowledge) to serve as a personal teacher, guide, or "friend." Such attention given to a lonely person is difficult to resist. One can easily do whatever mental gymnastics are needed to accept or at least go along with the teachings of a group where one starved for love and acceptance finds that need fulfilled.

A factor unique to men can be an emotional decision based on the organization's power structure. A man visiting a Kingdom Hall may observe the authority and prestige of the elders, desire it for himself, and discover that it is within his reach if only he will conform to the organizational requirements. This factor often comes into play in the case of black men who have found their advancement blocked at their place of employment or in the community at large, but who are able to become elders in the local Kingdom Hall (although blacks are seldom allowed to rise higher than that in the JW hierarchy). A similar motivation to join or remain with the sect sometimes occurs in the case of a henpecked husband; the male-dominated organization opens to him an area where he can step out from under his wife's control—much like a men's club or lodge.

Whatever the emotional need may be—whether for acceptance, companionship, prestige, or any other need—if the fulfillment of that need is the main force holding an individual in the Watchtower, that fact must be recognized by anyone attempting to effect liberation from the sect. Arguing doctrine or theology— even with the most persuasive logic—produces no results, because it is neither logic nor reason that is truly motivating the Witness. Like a love-struck teenage girl who hangs on her boyfriend's every word, the Witness who has found such emotional fulfillment in the organization is happy to applaud whatever the sect says.

In such cases the spell can usually be broken only when the honeymoon is over. After a while—perhaps a year or two after baptism—the new JW will come to be viewed as an ordinary member of the congregation. The courtship consisting of special treatment given to "students" and "new ones" will end. No longer will the other Witnesses go out of their way to be especially friendly, kind, and loving. In fact some of them may become hostile, mean and nasty—due to the pressure-cooker environment at Kingdom Hall. More than that, the organization will gradually reveal itself as a cold, demanding taskmaster. The new Witness may feel like a newlywed who wakes up one morning to the realization that her husband no longer opens doors, brings flowers, or spends time holding her hand, but in fact has become harsh and abusive. Or the man who has attained a certain level of prestige may find that further advancement is blocked by prejudice or internal politics, or he may even find himself demoted due to some minor infraction of the rules.

If it happens abruptly, this change in itself may be enough to shock the individual into rethinking his or her religious connections. Usually, however, all outside ties have been broken before this, so the unhappy Witness has nowhere else to go and no one to turn to. Like the disillusioned newlywed who resigns herself to the drudgery of keeping house for an unloving husband, the JW feels compelled to keep up meeting attendance and door-to-door magazine sales for the organizational master.

But this need not be the case. The Witness is not legally married to the organization. And there can indeed be somewhere else to go and someone to turn to—*if* you have lovingly stuck by your JW wife, friend, or relative until now.

The earlier discussions may not have worked, the proofs you

presented may have been ignored, and the evidence you produced may have been discounted. The JW may have closed a blind eye and a deaf ear to every appeal to reason that you had to offer, because the sect's drawing power was emotional rather than reasonable. But now the emotional tables have turned. The Witness begins to realize that the organization is unloving and unlovable, while, by way of contrast, you have remained a loyal and faithful friend through it all.

If it is your wife who is in the Watchtower, she will begin to see things in a different perspective: You lost arguments, but did not lose your temper; you respected her beliefs, although she did not respect yours; you put up with her spending all that time at Kingdom Hall meetings and in the house-to-house work; while she dutifully repeated what the organization was *saying* about God's love, you were actually *demonstrating* it in the way you treated her. This can carry more weight than volumes of theological arguments or historical discussions. And, when the organization eventually does become abusive, the disillusioned Witness knows that she can turn to you.

Similarly, when it is a relative or friend who is involved, this assurance of finding love and acceptance somewhere outside the JW community is an important factor in their deciding to leave.

Besides reasoning a person out of false teachings and offering a different source for the fulfillment of emotional needs, it is also vital to provide a spiritual alternative. The average person who joined the Jehovah's Witnesses did so, at least in part, because he or she had been reaching out for God. In the Beatitudes Jesus referred to such people as "the poor in spirit" or "those who feel their spiritual need" or "those who know their need of God" (Matt. 5:3, KJV, GOODSPEED, NEB). But, before they could come into a fulfilling relationship with God through Jesus Christ, someone came along and directed them to the Watchtower instead.

So, the new Witness came to see himself in a relationship with God illustrated by the organizational chart reproduced in chapter 11. Jehovah God was at the top of the corporate structure, and the individual was at the bottom. In between were multiple layers of committees and overseers—a hierarchy too vast to number. Personal prayer was allowed, but God's direction, instruction, and salvation could come only through the Watchtower Society. So the Witness was convinced of having a relationship with the Almighty through "God's visible organization." Commanding his unquestioning obedience, the organization became his *lord*; promising him salvation, it became his *savior*; and giving him a relationship with God, it was his *mediator*.

It was, however, a counterfeit. All of these titles and functions properly belong to Jesus Christ. He is the Lord and Savior and the Mediator revealed in the Bible. He is the One who said, "I am the way, the truth, and the life: no man cometh unto the Father, but by me" (John 14:6 KJV). So, the way to fill a JWs spiritual need is to point him to Jesus Christ.

How can this be accomplished? Unfortunately some well-meaning Christians try to do it by arguing the deity of Christ and the doctrine of the Trinity. But that puts a nearly insurmountable obstacle in the way. Also, imparting these scriptural truths falls more under the category of reasoning with the Witness to fulfill his rational needs and to correct his doctrines. *His spiritual need for a relationship with God is a different matter and should be considered separately.*

For example there are unsaved clergymen and theologians who can explain Christ's deity and trinitarian doctrine with great precision, but who are spiritually empty because they lack a personal relationship with the Lord. Many who were once in that condition have surprised laymen with their testimonies after coming to Christ. We want to avoid the mistake of teaching theology *instead* of leading the ex-JW to Christ.

Start out showing how the Watchtower Society has usurped the place of the Messiah in his role as Lord, Savior and Mediator. Persuade your loved one to put aside the Watchtower books and start reading the New Testament, especially the Gospels containing the words of Christ—preferably in a version other than the *New World Translation*. Encourage looking to Jesus for direction, instruction, and salvation. Show from Scripture that Christians can talk to Jesus, confident of his loving concern for them (Acts 7:59, 60; 1 Cor. 1:2; 2 Cor. 12:7-9; John 14:12-14). In this area your own example may carry more weight than anything you could possibly say.

The important thing is to help your loved one decide to follow Jesus Christ instead of continuing to follow a man-made organization. Correcting his or her theology is a separate issue. Remember that the twelve apostles were all Jewish when they began to follow Jesus. They started out holding various opinions as to who he was, but they all learned as they observed and interacted with him. It took doubting Thomas months—perhaps a couple of years as a follower of Jesus—before he could finally confess the resurrected Christ as "My Lord and my God!" (John 20:28). Since it may take your JW loved one as long as it took Thomas, ask God's help for you to be as patient with your loved one as He is.

Yes, patience is needed, because it takes time for people to rethink their entire religious outlook. But time is on your side. Statistics reveal that many who join the Jehovah's Witnesses drop out again after a few years. Tens of thousands are 'disfellowshiped' annually for violating some rule or policy. Some disassociate themselves by formally resigning from the sect. And others simply stop attending meetings and drift away. When I was an elder, I can remember fellow elders discussing the "revolving-door effect"; converts were coming in the front door, while others went out the back door of the Kingdom Hall. (But, since the influx was greater than the outflow, the group continued to grow.) The Watchtower's published statistics for 1971 through 1981 showed over 1,700,000 new members added through baptism, but a net gain of only 737,241 active Witnesses. So, roughly one million quit during that ten-year period (*Los Angeles Times*, 1/30/82). The organization has tightened its control since then, making it more difficult for members to leave. But there is still good reason to hope that a loved one who joins the Watchtower will not be in it for a lifetime.

But a lot will depend on your being there at the right time—not only with the right words to say and with convincing evidence to back you up, but also with a loving heart and a personal relationship with God. You will need to offer an alternative that will satisfy the individual's rational, emotional, and spiritual needs.

(*See* chapter 16 and the Appendix for further discussion of rehabilitation and a list of helpful resources.)

13

Can This Marriage Be Saved?

Of the men who have phoned or written me after their wives converted to the Jehovah's Witnesses, many have stated that they are seeking a divorce, that they are now living apart, or that they fear a separation is imminent. Can a marriage be saved, when one member becomes a JW? Or, if the bond is that between a parent and a grown child, between close relatives, or simply between friends, does the fact that one party has joined the Witnesses automatically spell doom for the relationship? Our discussion in this chapter will focus primarily on the situation of a married couple, but the suggestions offered can be beneficially applied to save other friendships as well.

Close communication and intimate sharing of thoughts and feelings enrich a marriage, drawing a couple together. But this rapport is difficult to achieve when the worldview of one mate is a world apart from that of the other. A religious split between husband and wife can be truly painful. Scripture speaks of a married couple as "one flesh" (Matt. 19:5, 6 KJV). What closer relationship could there be than that? A husband is counseled to love his wife as his own body (Eph. 5:28). So when mates start to go each their separate way religiously, it is like a person's left leg going in one direction while the right leg tries to go off in another direction—very uncomfortable!

Religiously mixed marriages are often successful where both parties are adherents of mainstream religious bodies. But exclusivist groups such as the Jehovah's Witnesses inject extra tension into the relationship. In part this is due to the hostility with which the sect regards outsiders and the hostility with which outsiders respond to the sect. Also at issue are some of the JWs more extreme positions, especially as they relate to children of the marriage. Added to that, there is the busy schedule of activities that the Witness must maintain without the mate.

There is certainly plenty of potential for marriage problems, but the first factor that needs to be examined honestly is the motives of the parties involved. All too often the new religion is simply an excuse used by a mate who had already wanted to end the marriage and who has finally found a "respectable" reason for doing so. It may be that the one who has joined the Witnesses has done so knowing this will be the last straw that will convince the spouse to depart—or perhaps sensing that the Kingdom Hall will provide a supportive atmosphere for leaving an unbeliever. Then again, it may be the non-Witness who feels that friends will understand his leaving a wife who has now joined a cult, whereas they might not sympathize were he to admit that he has simply lost interest in the marriage.

So, the new religion sometimes becomes a scapegoat for the party on either side who really wants to get a divorce anyway—for other reasons. If this is the case, nothing that can be said or done about Jehovah's Witnesses will have any effect on the situation. The religious issue is just a smokescreen hiding the genuine problem. If you perceive that this describes either you or your mate, the best step to take would be to seek professional help—preferably a secular marriage counselor acceptable to both parties—and to work at resolving the real obstacles, rather than allow either party to excuse himself and deceive others with the religious scapegoat.

But now suppose that it really *is* the religious difference that is at issue and that imperils the marriage. It should be noted that Christians, who believe in the Bible rather than *The Watchtower*, find no divine injunction to divorce a mate who joins a false religion. To the contrary, Scripture encourages the Christian to remain married: . . . "If any brother has a wife who is not a believer and she is willing to live with him, he must not divorce her. And if a woman has a husband who is not a believer and he is willing to live with her, she must not divorce him" (1 Cor. 7:12, 13 NIV). Unfortunately, immature Christians sometimes see matters differently and actually encourage separation from a JW mate.

Of course problems can be expected. The wife may feel obligated to preach Watchtower doctrine to her husband, whether he wants to hear it or not. Likewise he may harangue his wife with strident lectures about the organization's false teachings and harmful practices. In either case, if the listener responds in kind, the resulting argument tends to escalate in loudness and in bitterness. This, in turn, leads to such frustration on both sides that they stop speaking to each other on that subject—if not ceasing communication altogether.

But, if you are a Christian who realizes that God "hates divorce" (Mal. 2:16 NIV), there are ways that you can make your marriage work, even though your mate has become a Jehovah's Witness and seems determined to remain one.

First of all, before we look at methods for obtaining cooperation from your spouse, you would do well to look at yourself and how you fit into the picture. If you see self-pity or belligerence in the mirror, it is important to work at eliminating it, since it can be as destructive of the marriage as anything your mate could do. Ask yourself if self-pity is truly justified. Don't marriage partners pledge faithfulness "for better or for worse, in sickness and in health"? Aren't there many who find themselves with a mate who has become "worse" in areas far more distressing than a difference of religion? Moreover, isn't it true that "it takes two to tango" in most marital disputes?

Unless your spouse is absolutely determined to end the marriage, you can do a lot on your part to make it work and to keep it peaceful. The Proverbs tell us that, "Without wood a fire goes out" (Prov. 26:20 NIV). If you avoid adding fuel to the fire, arguments over religion may not flare up as often. If it becomes apparent that your mate does not want to listen to anything you have to say on religious subjects, you need not feel an obligation to keep pushing the issue. This would not constitute surrender or defeat on your part, but would simply show that you accept the wisdom of the apostle Peter's counsel, where he wrote, "Likewise you wives, be submissive to your husbands, so that some, though they do not obey the word, may be won without a word by the behavior of their wives, when they see your reverent and chaste behavior" (1 Peter 3:1, 2 RSV). Peter wrote that advice to Christian women who were married to non-Christians in ancient Pontus, Galatia, Cappadocia, Asia, and Bithynia. Their husbands may have been Jews hostile to Christianity, or they may have been pagan idolaters or Roman emperor-worshipers. And, yet, Peter recommended good behavior, rather than argumentative discussions, as the way to win them over. Likewise in your marriage to a Jehovah's Witness: if she does not want to listen to your words on religion, preach to her "without a word" by your loving conduct and tender affection.

But there are certain things about the organization's teachings on marriage that it will be helpful for you to know. Believe it or not, the Watchtower teaches basically the same approach outlined by Peter in the Bible—except it is the Witness who views you as the "unbelieving mate." You can help eliminate religious arguments by pointing out Peter's counsel to your mate, and asking if she agrees with it. (She will have to say *Yes*. Then she is obliged to try to win you over without a word of argument.) But be sure to do this without pointing the finger at her, making her feel that the problem has been all her fault. Accept at least some of the blame yourself.

While local JW elders sometimes take it upon themselves to encourage separation from an unbelieving mate, the official policy from Brooklyn headquarters is to do everything possible to keep the marriage together. Divorce with remarriage is allowed only if the non-Witness engages in sexual immorality with another person, although it is often assumed that a non-JW who spends nights away from home is doing this. A permanent separation is also permitted if the unbelieving mate moves out of the home or becomes abusive to the point of endangering the Witness's life, health or well-being.

Notice that religious difference alone is not listed among the acceptable grounds for separation. However, JW elders may interpret preventing your wife from getting to Kingdom Hall meetings or attempting to persuade her to leave the religion as endangering her spiritual well-being. In such a case they may advise her to leave you.

Ultimately, though, it will come down to the two of you. Do you both really want to stay together? Then you can make it work. Many others have done so. How? Basically by applying the biblical principles outlined above for a good marriage—

principles which Christians and Jehovah's Witnesses generally agree upon, and which form the basis of most marriage counselors' advice.

Sometimes it is said that marriage is a fifty-fifty proposition. But a person determined to carry out his or her marriage vows will find that there are times when it is necessary to give 100 percent, expecting nothing in return. The result, though, from 100-percent giving is usually a better return than when one insists upon giving no more than 50 percent and demands 50 percent in return.

What if there are children involved? Is there any alternative to divorce court and a bitter custody battle? This is one of the points that will be considered in our next chapter.

14

When Children Are Involved

Seeing a child in the grip of a cult can be as painful as seeing the little one carried off by a kidnapper. If it is a neighbor's child that your youngsters play with, the pain is real enough; but if it is your own children who are in the custody of an estranged mate, bent on raising them in a cult, it may seem almost unendurable.

Yet every Kingdom Hall is full of children. Many of these have one parent who is not a Jehovah's Witness, and virtually all of them have at least one grandparent, uncle or aunt outside the sect. The non-Witness relatives of such children suffer much distress over their fate, and with good cause. Children raised as JWs have a difficult road to travel.

Infants can be heard crying and toddlers fussing during all the meetings. One reason for this is that the Watchtower makes no provision for such things as nursery, children's church, or Sunday school—no youth-oriented programs at all for little ones to attend while parents participate in the regular meetings. Instead, the youngsters are required to sit and pay attention as speakers deliver lectures or conduct question-and-answer sessions using *Watchtower* study articles.

And if the children of Jehovah's Witnesses have a hard time at Kingdom Hall, they have an even worse time at school, where they are required to refuse to salute the flag, or to stand for the national anthem, and to avoid participating in holiday-related activities such as coloring Thanksgiving turkeys or singing Christmas carols. In the early grades, where much attention is given to holidays and children's birthdays, this can mean that a Witness child is excluded from the activities of the rest of the class at least once every week, and daily when it comes to saluting the flag.

And, of course, the plight of a JW youngster becomes a life-and-death matter when need arises for a blood transfusion and a Witness parent or parents refuse to allow it. (Although most hospitals nowadays have contingency plans to obtain a court order in such cases.)

No wonder, then, that disagreement over raising the children is a common factor in Witness-related divorces, with bitter fights ensuing over custody and visitation rights.

In addition to *Watchtower* articles giving pointers to both custodial and noncustodial parents as to how best to handle issues related to visitation rights, Brooklyn headquarters also makes available to its followers and their attorneys a collection of favorable court precedents, as well as a sixty-four page booklet titled *Preparing for Child Custody Cases*. The latter helps them anticipate hostile questions they should expect under cross-examination and during psychological evaluation. Very clearly, the Watchtower Society is prepared to wage war for the children of its members.

What about the other side? What about parents, grandparents, uncles, aunts, neighbors, and others who observe children in the custody of Jehovah's Witnesses? And what about a Christian husband in a religiously mixed marriage who must contemplate raising the children together with his JW wife, or fighting her for custody?

As to neighbors and relatives outside the immediate family circle the answer is painful but simple. Courts generally rule that they have no say in the religious upbringing of other people's children. As difficult as it may be, they must remain mere onlookers, at least as far as legal rights are concerned. Naturally there may be opportunities to make contact and to impart some religious information or assurances of affection, but these are not guaranteed. The only avenue that is always open is that of prayer to the heavenly Father of us all, remembering that Christ said, "Let the little children come to me, and do not hinder them, for the kingdom of heaven belongs to such as these" (Matt. 19:14 NIV).

Parents of course are in a position to exercise legal as well as God-given rights in connection with their children. The Watchtower Society instructs its followers to do all in their power to raise the children as Witnesses. But in a religiously mixed marriage much will depend on the two individuals involved. What actually occurs will be a product of the interaction of their personalities and will reflect each one's love, determination, wisdom and reasonableness. I have seen cases where a custody battle reached the court before the infant was weaned, and other cases where husband and wife managed to stay together, to stay in love, and to raise a family of four or more children to maturity. So no one can say that a certain course of events is inevitable.

If the children are the main concern, my observation is that family breakup does far more lasting harm to them than exposure to the Watchtower while growing up. Even in cases of simple secular divorce, where there is no religious issue involved, it has been well documented that the children suffer long-term emotional harm. This is especially so when they themselves are pulled this way and that by estranged parents, battling for their custody and their affections. Adding a religious issue to this only further complicates the situation from the child's point of view. Studies have proven that children tend to blame themselves for the parental rift, and now they must contend with the thought of offending God as well.

When speaking of the effect of divorce on children, some have said that it "tears them apart." The Bible tells of a custody battle in which that was nearly the case, quite literally:

> Now two prostitutes came to the king and stood before him. One of them said, "My lord, this woman and I live in the same house. I had a baby while she was there with me. The third day after my child was born, this woman also had a baby. We were alone; there was no one in the house but the two of us.
>
> "During the night this woman's son died because she lay on him. So she got up in the middle of the night and took my son from my side while I your servant was asleep. She put him by her breast and put her dead son by my breast. The next morning, I got up to nurse my son—and he was dead! But when I looked at him closely in the morning light, I saw that it wasn't the son I had borne."

The other woman said, "No! The dead one is yours; the living one is mine." And so they argued before the king.

The king said, "This one says, 'My son is alive and your son is dead,' while that one says, 'No! Your son is dead and mine is alive.'"

Then the king said, "Bring me a sword." So they brought a sword for the king. He then gave an order: "Cut the living child in two and give half to one and half to the other."

The woman whose son was alive was filled with compassion for her son and said to the king, "Please, my lord, give her the living baby! Don't kill him!"

But the other said, "Neither I nor you shall have him. Cut him in two!"

Then the king gave his ruling: "Give the living baby to the first woman. Do not kill him; she is his mother" (1 Kings 3:16-27 NIV).

Besides demonstrating the wisdom of King Solomon, this account also pointed out that a loving parent might be more willing to surrender a child to another, rather than see the child torn in two. Similarly, some Christian fathers have decided that it is better to let the children be exposed to the mother's Jehovah's Witness beliefs than to tear the little ones apart through a divorce and custody battle.

Whether the family stays together or not, in either case it can be painful for the non-Witness to see his or her children exposed to Watchtower teachings. Yet this is usually unavoidable. So the real question becomes: how should the Christian mate react? Should he tell the little ones that their mother is bad? that she is in a cult? that she is telling them lies about God? The mother may tell them such things about the non-Witness father. But then again, she may not. And if she does, what purpose would be served by responding in kind?

Ideally, for the sake of the children, the parents will be able to reach some sort of compromise. Perhaps they will decide, at least while the children are very young, to emphasize the points that they hold in common, rather than those where they diverge. Perhaps they can agree to disagree agreeably, letting the older children know that they hold differing opinions on some points, but that they still love each other. In cases where parents have taken this approach, it has worked well.

Actually, it is not the lack of agreement between parents that disturbs children, but rather the bitterness and hostility that all too often accompany it. Children are accustomed to lack of agreement and can live with it. They believe that ice cream is better for you, while their parents believe that spinach is. They believe that a messy room looks great, while their parents believe toys should be put away. And they may even grasp that mother believes a vacation in the mountains is best, while father believes in the beach. Disagreement does not harm children, but disagreeable behavior does.

Suppose, though, that the Witness mother tells the children that she is right, that the father is wrong, and even attempts to poison their minds against him? There is no easy answer, but responding with the same sort of attacks against her is not productive. In such circumstances the Christian parent should find some comfort in two facts: (1) Children are very perceptive and look at much more than just the words spoken to size up a situation; and (2) their long-range interests may dictate a different response than what seems immediately appropriate.

Besides what mother *says* about father, the children notice also how mother acts and how father acts. They can tell whether he loves them and their mother, and over a period of time, they will make their own value judgment on what mother says. Even though they may not verbalize it, the children will know which parent is the peacemaker, which one is firm but loving, which one truly has their interests at heart. Hopefully, both will. But if one does not, the children will discover that.

Another reason for hope, in the long term, is the success rate of Jehovah's Witnesses with their children. The failure rate would be a more appropriate way of putting it. The experience of being raised at Kingdom Hall tends to convince young people *not* to remain Jehovah's Witnesses when they reach the age of decision. As an elder for eight years in a local JW congregation I had to deal with case after case of teenagers breaking the rules. By the time they reached their teen years, most children in the congregation were living a double life—one personality among their friends at school and in the neighborhood, and a put-on Witness personality at Kingdom Hall and in front of their parents. When they turned eighteen, or when they moved out of the home, they ceased involvement with the sect altogether.

It is *not* as though it were a life-or-death matter to safeguard children from exposure to Watchtower teachings during their formative years. Such exposure actually seems to immunize many youngsters against becoming Witnesses when they grow up. On the other hand, some youngsters who have been kept from a JW parent may develop an unhealthy curiosity about that one's religion, leading them to try it out when they become of age.

According to the inspired counsel of 1 Corinthians 7:14 a Christian need not fear for children in a religiously mixed home, regardless of whether the unbelieving parent is a pagan Corinthian or a Jehovah's Witness: "For the unbelieving husband has been sanctified through his wife, and the unbelieving wife has been sanctified through her believing husband. Otherwise your children would be unclean, but as it is, they are holy" (NIV).

15

Warning: The Life You Save May Be Your Own

Setting out to rescue someone from a cult is serious business. It should not be approached lightly. Not only can a poorly planned attempt leave the cultist more hopelessly entrenched, but it can also put the would-be rescuer at risk.

"Who, me?" some readers may be scoffing to themselves. "Why, I would *never* become a Jehovah's Witness!" And I am sure that they are sincere and fully convinced in that confidence. But, so was I when I spoke those identical words early in 1968. A few months later I went on to study with the Witnesses, was baptized as a full-fledged member the following spring, and remained in the organization for thirteen years.

"For false Christs and false prophets will arise," Jesus warned, "and show great signs and wonders, so as to lead astray, if possible, even the elect" (Matt. 24:24 RSV). Overconfidence has no place in dealing with such powerful forces. I have known personally a number of people who had originally set out to expose the Watchtower's deceptions, only to end up fully deceived themselves. Some of these were husbands seeking to liberate their wives from the sect, but even trained cult fighters are not immune. One such individual who represented himself as a "born-again, spirit-filled Christian" was on the staff of a counter-cult ministry when he allowed Jehovah's Witnesses to start a study with him, so that he could lead them to Christ. Instead, he was led into the Watchtower, publicly renouncing his Christian faith and becoming fully involved at Kingdom Hall. (He eventually came to his senses again and left the group, but only after many months of misery.)

In another case a Baptist deacon followed his wife out of the church and into the Watchtower organization. He remained in it until his death, years later.

One of the dozens of individuals I personally led into the sect was a Lutheran Sunday-school teacher and treasurer of the local Lutheran church. This man was skeptical at first, but soon became convinced I was teaching him "the Truth." He resigned his position and membership in the Lutheran church and began attending Kingdom Hall.

So it is not wise to boast, as I myself once did, that "it could never happen to me." Recognizing your own vulnerability will be a good first step toward safeguarding yourself. The second step should be to enlist the aid of others—preferably someone knowledgeable and experienced. But if such an expert is not available, at least get some friends to be prayer partners with you. Share your research with them. Let them know when you plan to meet with your JW friend and what you plan to discuss. Then immediately after the encounter, regardless of whether it turns out to be a success or a disappointment, see your friends again to discuss with them what happened. Keep them fully informed of your efforts. Should you start to fall for some deceptive cultic argument, they will be able to discuss it with you right away and give you a different perspective.

Recognizing that there is strength in numbers, be sure not to fall into a trap where the odds are stacked against you—such as a discussion with a Witness friend or loved one who "just happens" to be accompanied by an elder or two, a circuit overseer, or another more experienced JW. Although you may have been practicing swordplay in the backyard, that does not mean that you are ready to take on the Three Musketeers. Yet that is exactly the sort of match you would be up against in such an encounter. If you find yourself unexpectedly facing such overwhelming odds, simply excuse yourself saying that you will be happy to meet with your Witness friend alone on another occasion.

Be sure, too, that you yourself are strong enough for the challenge. This involves more than simply being fully prepared to speak on the Witnesses; the strength of your own faith must be capable of sustaining you under test. Besides knowing what is wrong with Watchtower doctrine, you must also know what *you* believe, and why. The tactic JWs are taught to use when under attack is a strong counterattack, aimed at what they perceive to be your weakest spot.

Counterfeit money can not stand up to a comparison with the real thing, but someone who spends all his time looking at phony bills and never sees real ones could be fooled by a good fake. Likewise with religion: if you are going to do battle with a cult, it is vital that you spend time sharing in worship and fellowship with real Christians. Also draw close to God in prayer. Counterfeit Christianity is pale and flimsy in comparison with the real thing. If your faith is solidly founded on biblical knowledge, and you know God personally through a close, personal relationship with Jesus Christ, you will be able to march into this or any other battle fearing nothing.

16

Afterwork: Gradual Rehabilitation

With so much effort directed toward freeing your loved one from bondage, once that goal is reached, there may be a tendency to breathe a sigh of relief and to say, "Whew! I'm glad that's over and done with." But your work is not finished yet. The one you helped escape will also need help to return to a normal life.

Some people exit a cult like a tightly coiled spring sprung loose from a restraint. The spring bounces all over the place and finally falls to the floor vibrating all over; likewise, the excultist bounces from group to group, until finally collapsing a nervous wreck. Some set out on a search for another organization to replace the one proved false. Others become bitter toward God, religion, and anything else that reminds them of the past. A few even turn to alcohol or drugs to escape the complexities of the real world.

Many ex-Witnesses appear to be living a normal life but actually suffer from haunting memories, nagging doubts, unsettled questions, and suppressed fears. They instinctively feel that no one but another former JW would understand, so they keep these troubling thoughts to themselves, continuing to be troubled by them.

Seldom does anyone exit a cult without emotional wounds, spiritual scars, and a sense of disorientation. And the longer the person has spent in the group, the longer the healing and renormalization process can be expected to take. This is especially true of Jehovah's Witnesses. They were slowly taught to think like JWs before they were baptized into the organization, and once they are brought out of the organization they must slowly learn to think normally again.

"Time heals all wounds," someone may quote the popular saying. "Just give her time, and she'll be back to her old self again." There is some truth to that, of course. Watchtower leaders themselves know that constant indoctrination is needed to maintain a strong hold on their followers. Missing meetings is a sin, and staying away from Kingdom Hall for an extended vacation is tantamount to apostasy—because the message constantly repeated at the meetings begins to fade from the brain as soon as the foot hits the street. That is why Witnesses are expected to attend meetings Tuesday and Thursday evenings and Sunday mornings; go from house to house with the group on Saturday mornings, Sunday afternoons, and at other opportunities during the week; spend Monday, Wednesday, and Saturday evenings preparing lessons for upcoming meetings, and use other available time to conduct studies with family members and prospective converts. Any departure from this schedule allows room for independent thinking to develop. And abandoning the program altogether, even for a short period of time, almost always results in leaving the organization.

So after a person has formally quit the sect, each passing day does provide fresh food for thought, pushing the old memories further back in the mind. But time alone is not a cure-all. Like knots in a rope, each tangled reasoning or troubled thought must be dealt with individually.

Someone may have rejected the organization but may still think it wrong to accept a blood transfusion, or may feel guilty eating a rare steak with juices on the plate. Another ex-JW may feel uncomfortable around an American flag. I have seen terror on the face of a former Witness entering a church building for the first time. Many hesitate to vote in an election. Some worry constantly about questions relating to God, the afterlife, and the nature of true Christianity.

An observer who has never been immersed in a cult may be able to brush such matters aside, telling the ex-JW, "Oh! That's just a lot of silly nonsense. Come on! You don't have to believe that anymore; you're out of the Watchtower now. Just forget all that stuff!"

The former Witness may manage to smile and respond, "Okay! You're right!" He or she may even go ahead and do the act in question, such as standing for the national anthem, but the problem actually remains and in fact gets worse, because now it is suppressed and is compounded by a guilty conscience. Unless the twisted reasoning is patiently untwisted, point by point, real healing does not occur. It is like a splinter that is not removed but instead is treated with painkiller, disinfectant, and a Band-Aid. It may seem to be cured, but the pain will recur until the splinter is actually extracted.

Time and again I have encountered men and women who had left the Watchtower years earlier, but who were still being troubled by problems common to those who are just now coming out. Why? Because the root of their problems had never yet been fully addressed; or because the persons who tried to help them were not really qualified and did not get the job done.

Except for rare individuals who have received special training or who have unique insight, it usually takes another ex-JW to help a former Witness. Most of those who were troubled for years after leaving the Watchtower did not find relief until they finally encountered an ex-JW support group, made friends with another ex-Witness, or read literature written by someone who had gone through the same ordeal.

The reason for this is that the indoctrination formerly received on a continual basis, although now rejected, has still left behind a residue of peculiar ideas and thought patterns. As a result, ex-Witnesses start off with different assumptions than ordinary folk. For example, a roomful of people may listen to a minister preach the gospel. Quite a few of those who hear the message may accept Jesus Christ as their Lord and Savior and "come forward" when invited. But the ex-JW in the audience remains unmoved, or even confused, because what he heard did not make sense to him. In his mind, Jesus is an angel—Michael the Archangel, to be exact—because this particular aspect of Watchtower teaching had never been cleared up for him. So the words the minister spoke were sufficient to convince others in the audience, because they shared certain common assumptions. But the ex-Witness had something altogether different in his mind, and the minister's message failed to deal with it.

A few people manage to deprogram themselves upon leaving the organization; such individuals are usually readers who spend a lot of time alone with the Bible and with other books that help them gain a new world view. Some married couples deprogram each other by discussing what they used to believe and what to believe now, while each one receives fresh insight through reading and through contact with workmates or neighbors. They share these new thoughts together, gradually stripping themselves of their former belief structure. But all ex-Witnesses need some form of outside help to successfully shed the mental baggage they have been saddled with by their former mentors.

If you are engaged in helping someone in this position, then you should be prepared to assist this thought transformation. Transporting a person physically out of a Kingdom Hall and into a church is a major accomplishment. But the changes taking place *inside* the person are what really count. And those changes take place gradually over a long period of time. A lot of patient assistance is needed, both before and after the break with the sect.

You will be able to initiate some of the discussion required to help a former Witness rethink his or her beliefs. But many other points will have to be addressed when they happen to come up in the individual's mind; you will need to make yourself available to be called upon at such times.

You can also provide supplementary assistance by putting the ex-JW in touch with others who have gone through a similar experience. In some localities there are support groups for former cultists, some specifically for ex-Jehovah's Witnesses. In recent years ex-JWs have been regularly holding annual conventions in California, Florida, and Pennsylvania, besides occasional gatherings in large cities elsewhere.

But caution must be exercised in selecting such association, since in some cases, persons who are only half out of the Watchtower get together to *perpetuate* their shared beliefs. A few individuals who are all just leaving the sect at the same time may find each other and get together for mutual support; they all need help, but there is no one among them competent to give help. The blind end up leading the blind. They share the same problem, but none of them has yet found the solution. The result is that the group stagnates, functioning as an entity separate from the Watchtower, but retaining many of the strange notions that its members still share in common. Such a group will not be able to help your friend.

So before putting your friend in touch with a support group, or before passing on a book or tape, you would do well first to assure yourself that the group, author, or speaker is truly free.

For those in areas distant from wholesome ex-JW association, there are newsletters and fellowships formed through the mail. And there are books of testimonies and admonition written by former Witnesses.

For assistance in finding valid support groups and resources, see the Appendix.

Appendix:
Resources and Support Groups

Because the person battling the Watchtower needs all the help he or she can get, we list here a number of publications, ministries and local support groups that may prove to be of assistance.

Books

Bussell, Harold L., *Unholy Devotion: Why Cults Lure Christians* (Zondervan Publishing House, 1983)

Chretien, Leonard & Marjorie, *Witnesses of Jehovah* (Harvest House Publishers, 1988)

Franz, Raymond V., *Crisis of Conscience* (Commentary Press, 1983)

Hassan, Steven, *Combatting Cult Mind Control* (Park Street Press, 1988)

Hewitt, Joe, *I Was Raised a Jehovah's Witness* (Accent Books, 1979)

Magnani, Duane, and Arthur Barrett, *The Watchtower Files* (Bethany House Publishers, 1985)

Penton, M. James, *Apocalypse Delayed: The Story of Jehovah's Witnesses* (University of Toronto Press, 1985)

Reed, David A., *Jehovah's Witnesses Answered Verse by Verse* (Baker Book House, 1986)

Sire, James W., *Scripture Twisting: 20 Ways the Cults Misread the Bible* (InterVarsity Press, 1980)

Note: There are many other excellent books on Jehovah's Witnesses and cults in general. Those listed above are a few that we believe the average reader with a loved one in the sect will find most helpful. A number of other useful books, booklets and newsletters have been self-published by the various ministries noted below.

Ministries and Support Groups

Acts 1:8 Outreach, P.O. Box 1300, Port Ewen, NY 12466. 24-hour message for JWs (914-338-8644).

Alpha & Omega Ministries, P.O. Box 47041, Phoenix, AZ 85068. Newsletter, booklets, tracts, traveling speakers, 24-hour recorded message for JWs (602-266-2597).

Bethel Ministries, P.O. Box 3818, Manhattan Beach, CA 90266. Newsletter, books, tapes, videos, traveling speaker, 24-hour recorded message for JWs (213-546-2937).

Comments from the Friends, P.O. Box 840, Stoughton, MA 02072. Newsletter, books, tapes, videos, counseling, traveling speaker, 24-hour recorded message for JWs (508-584-4467), computerized list of local contacts. [This is the ministry of David A. Reed, author of this book.]

Good News Defenders, P.O. Box 8007, La Jolla, CA 92038. Traveling speakers, film, videos, books, tapes, tracts.

Gospel Truth Ministries, P.O. Box 4148, Brockton, MA 02403. Newsletter, free lending library of books, tapes, videos.

Jesus Loves the Lost, P.O. Box 707, Easton, PA 18042. 24-hour recorded message for JWs (215-250-0643).

MacGregor Ministries, P.O. Box 73, Balfour, B.C. V0G 1C0, Canada. Newsletter, books, tapes, tracts, traveling speakers, 24-hour recorded message for JWs (604-274-3927).

Make Sure Ministries, P.O. Box 2937, Boca Raton, FL 33427. Support group, counseling, Spanish language also.

Make Sure Ministries, P.O. Box 24, New Providence, PA 17560. Support group, traveling speakers.

Ministerios Alfa y Omega, P.O. Box 373, Roosevelt, NY 11575. Spanish language newsletter and 24-hour recorded message for JWs (516-379-8167 Spanish language).

Mount Carmel Outreach, P.O. Box 756, Rock Falls, IL 61071. Traveling speakers, 24-hour recorded message for JWs (815-625-3678)

Personal Freedom Outreach, P.O. Box 26062, St Louis, MO 63136. Newsletter, books, tapes, videos, traveling speakers.

Personal Freedom Outreach—East, R.D. 3, Box 127, Kunkletown, PA 18058. Traveling speaker, support group, annual ex-Witness convention.

Pioneer Ministries, P.O. Box 554, Timberville, VA 22853. Support group, 24-hour messages for JWs (703-459-8425 and 703-896-6403).

Tutors for Christ, P.O. Box 54654, Lexington, KY 40555. Support group, traveling speakers.

Watchman Fellowship, P.O. Box 74091, Birmingham, AL 35253. Newsletter, books, tracts, tapes, videos, traveling speakers, 24-hour message for JWs (205-871-0700).

Witness, Inc., P.O. Box 597, Clayton, CA 94517. Books, tracts, traveling speakers.

Note: Those listed above represent only a sampling of the many local ministries and support groups—primarily the largest, those staffed by former Witnesses, and those most likely to be able to refer inquirers to sources of help closer to home. For a more complete list of such ministries and support groups, please see the *Directory of Cult Research Organizations*, published annually by Cornerstone Press, 4707 N. Malden St., Chicago, IL 60640.

I have a computerized listing of thousands of contacts across the United States. If you wish to find help in your locality, or if you have questions or comments concerning this book, you may write David A. Reed, c/o Comments from the Friends, P.O. Box 840, Stoughton, Massachusetts 02072.

Index

Scripture Index